ANSWERING 911

Answering

Life in the Hot Seat

CAROLINE BURAU

Borealis Books is an imprint of the Minnesota Historical Society Press.
www.borealisbooks.org

The Minnesota Historical Society Press is a member of the Association of American University Presses.

Manufactured in the
United States of America

10 9 8 7 6 5 4 3

∞ The paper used in this publication meets the minimum requirements of the American National Standard for Information Sciences—Permanence for Printed Library Materials, ANSI Z39.48-1984.

International Standard
Book Number
ISBN 13: 978-0-87351-602-0
ISBN 10: 0-87351-602-8

Library of Congress
Cataloging-in-Publication Data

Burau, Caroline
Answering 911 : life in the hot seat / Caroline Burau.
p. cm.
ISBN-13: 978-0-87351-569-6 (cloth : alk. paper)
ISBN-10: 0-87351-569-2 (cloth : alk. paper)
1. Burau, Caroline, 1973–
2. Police dispatchers—United States—Biography.
3. Assistance in emergencies—United States.
4. Telephone—Emergency reporting systems.
I. Title.
II. Title: Answering nine-one-one.
HV7911.B85A3 2006
384.6′4—dc22 2006009896

For M. & D., who made me,

And for Jim & M., who make me better

ANSWERING 911

ANSWERING 911

What It's Like

Maybe you and I have already spoken, but we didn't exchange names. You probably told me yours, but mine never came up. You may have yelled at me, or begged me to hurry, or passed out in my ear. You may have told me something really personal. I might remember it, or I might not. I may glance at your house as I drive to the store or to pick up my daughter, but I won't slow down. I don't necessarily want to know people's secrets, I just do.

If I write about you sometime, it's nothing to get worried about. I've forgotten your name, or changed it, and I'm just getting it all out. If you left something with me, maybe I'm just trying to give it back. If I left something with you, I hope it was good. Maybe I was there when you had your worst day ever. Maybe it was my worst day too, until the next one.

One thing's for sure: If you saw me on the street, you would never know me. You couldn't thank me, if that's what you might want. You couldn't smack me in the face, either.

My family worried, when I left the newspaper, that I wasn't going to be a writer anymore. But the day after Dori Swanson died, I started writing about *it.* I had to tell someone about her, what she did to herself, and then what she did to me. I kept on writing because I wanted to do something to record all of the other Dori Swansons I was meeting in this new life of mine.

Maybe someday, I'll get it right. I'll explain what it's like to be on the receiving end of a shitty, insane, life-changing call, and I'll do it justice. I'll figure out how to make you understand what it's like to be staring at a crossword puzzle and trying to think of a six-letter word for "run rapidly" one minute, and the next, asking a twelve-year-old girl what kind of a gun her mother just used to blow her own head off. Someday I'll figure out how to make you feel it, and then maybe I'll win the Pulitzer Prize. Or maybe you'll hate me for it.

Every day that I sit down at a console in the 911 center, I tell myself that today could be the day. If I don't, I'll forget and get lazy. Today could be the day that I take a call that will change me a little bit forever. It could be the day that a bell gets rung that I can never un-ring. Someone could die in my ear today and take a piece of me with him. Someone could tell me something unimaginable, and I'll have to imagine it.

Still, I can relax. Statistically, it's probably not going

to happen *today*. What's likely *today* is that I'll watch a little TV and make a lot of small talk with the dispatcher at the console next to me. What's also likely is that I will become intimately familiar with whatever word game or crossword puzzle has been downloaded to my computer by some other dispatcher, and that even though I'll play it on and off for the next seven to eight hours, I'll still suck at it by the end of the shift.

There will be plenty of 911 calls, but most of them won't be anywhere near as interesting as most people believe.

"You're a 911 operator? Wow! I bet you've got some stories." I get that at parties a lot.

"Oh, yeah," I say. Then in the space where you would expect me to start telling one of those wildly interesting stories, I usually draw a blank and start sipping meaningfully on my Diet Coke.

The most interesting stories are also the saddest. And you only *think* you want to hear them until I tell them to you. Then you start sipping meaningfully on *your* Diet Coke and you don't know what to say.

They are the stories where mothers and fathers fail their children. They are the stories where friends and lovers do awful things to hurt each other because of drugs or alcohol, or worse, for no real reason at all. Or they are the fascinating ways that some people lose their grip on reality. Interesting? Yeah, but not amusing. And I don't always want to tell them to you at a party because I might try to make them amusing just because I think that's what you want to hear.

One night, surfing the Internet for books about 911 dispatching, I found a single book, meant to be funny, packed with wacky, real-life stories about 911. The lone review warned potential buyers that the book wasn't funny at all, just depressing.

But death and chaos aren't the only events that make the 911 phones ring. Most of the calls are actually pretty routine. By routine, I mean that they are routine to *us*. Maybe not to you, though.

"My husband slipped out of his wheelchair. Can somebody help me lift him?"

"Someone broke into my car."

"My 16-year-old son is smoking pot."

"My neighbors are shooting off fireworks again."

"Somebody egged my house!"

Those are the calls we get by the hundreds and thousands. It's hard to feel anything much for those people, not because they don't deserve it, but because there are so many. It's especially hard to listen to the ones who want to act like getting their cell phones stolen out of their cars is the BFD of the century. Listen, if you leave it on the seat in broad daylight with the doors unlocked, then get ready to kiss it goodbye. And don't expect me to cry a river over it either. Just give me your name, number and location so I can send out the cop, who will be equally apathetic, to take a report. And when the cop doesn't wail and gnash his or her teeth over your cell phone either, you'll think we're all a bunch of insensitive bastards. Think whatever you want, I guess. Just lock your door next time.

The problem is, if I cry over your cell phone, then I won't have anything left for the calls that need me. The night that Dori Swanson died, I cried. But I waited until the end of the shift.

"911?"

"*My mom just killed herself!*"

"How did she kill herself?"

"She shot herself. *Oh my God.*"

"Where's the gun?"

"It's in her hand."

"Is she still alive?"

"I don't think so. Oh God! No. She's dead."

"How old are you?"

"I'm twelve."

I would never trade places with the cops that had to go out to Dori Swanson's trailer that night. I would never say that I have a harder job than the medics who had to treat her dead body while her three kids wailed and screamed outside. I would never want to be the police chaplain who had to try to comfort them. But I will say this: At least they had a minute or two to get ready.

Three seconds ago, I had a chair under my ass and a word puzzle in my hand. Then the phone rings, and suddenly I have been transferred, shot out, struck in the chest.

I talk to the daughter, who is hysterical. Lots of people use the word "hysterical" when they really mean that a person is just very *upset.* My caller is hysterical.

Then I talk to her stepfather, who is neither upset nor hysterical.

"Is she breathing?" I ask.

"I'm not in the room with her," Dad tells me. "I don't want to be blamed for anything." Then, with me still on the line, Dad's cell phone rings. He sets me down and answers it. To whomever is on the line, he says, "Dori shot herself. . . . Yeah. Yeah, no shit. . . . I gotta go. Bye."

There are many people in the world just like this man. I never knew that until I took this job. The tough part, the longer you do this job, is remembering that most people *aren't* like him.

For the next four minutes, I try to convince Dad to keep his three children out of the room where their mother lies dying (or already dead). They can't help her; at this point they can only endanger themselves. Despite my efforts, all I hear are screams overlapping screams; I am no more in control of this scene than I am of the moon in the sky.

At last, the cops and medics arrive, call a Code 4 (meaning okay, for now), and just like that, I'm disconnected from 874 Langer Drive. It's like I've been dangling twenty feet in the air, hoping to be let down. Then somebody cuts my cord, and I'm bracing for the fall.

That's the moment I first notice that my body is on fire. I am completely *hot* from head to toe. Kristen, the lead dispatcher, stands up at her console and tells me I did a good job. She tells me I stayed calm.

I did? I don't remember.

My hands and face are burning. My head is thick. Though I quit smoking about three months ago, I bum a cigarette off someone and head outside. It's fifteen degrees out, and I don't take my coat.

The cigarette tastes like shit to me. It's been too long. I would put it out and go inside, but if I don't take at least a few more minutes out here in the cold, Kristen will probably send me back out. Just relax, she'll say. Take ten minutes. As if a full ten minutes is sufficient to wipe Dori Swanson's mess off me.

I think, *What a bitch.* Who does that? Who blows

their brains out in front of their kids? This is ridiculous. I never even met her. I gotta get back to work.

When I return to my seat, I'm hot and shivering at the same time.

The phone rings. I stare at the blinking line a moment before I pick it up. I remember a reporter I used to work with, before I worked at 911, who would look at his ringing desk phone and say, "What fresh hell awaits?"

If he only knew.

"911?"

"Hi. My neighbor's clarinet is keeping me up. It's 8:30 PM, for God's sake!"

"What's your name?"

"I mean, don't you think that's ridiculous?"

"Yes, ma'am. I do. What's your address?"

And so on, until it's time to go home.

Later, the shift is over and I'm sitting on my couch. I think of what it must be like at Dori Swanson's house. I envision a cramped mobile home, maybe one of those single-wide jobs with the rotting wooden siding and the redwood deck, about six by eight. I see the kids' bikes that never got put away for the winter, now partially snow-covered.

Outside of the fact that she lived in a trailer, I really don't know any of this. But I took the call; I'm involved. So I put myself there. I imagine it as it must have been, so I can grieve it, then maybe let it go.

Inside, I see the dirt-soaked beige carpet and the second-hand furniture of the Swanson family living room. I see the TV that's always on. I see the overflowing ashtrays, and the filth, and the empty box of wine the chaplain later told me that she drank that day. I see kids' drawings taped onto the harvest gold refrigerator. I see five lives that will never be the same. Six.

I see the bedroom where Dori killed herself, just briefly, but I don't stay there long. I wonder if what the cops saw at the scene is more or less horrifying than the image in my head.

I check my stepdaughter and my husband in their beds, asleep. I wait for my husband's chest to rise and then fall. I do the same with Lucy. I look around at my own family room, then at my kitchen. I scan Lucy's drawings on the white refrigerator door.

I never met Dori Swanson, but I wish she had found something worth living for in that trailer. I cry on the couch in my living room, so I won't have to cry in bed and wake my husband up.

I think about her boy, who is his early teens. The chaplain said he called her a bitch just before she died. We'll hear his name again, I'm sure. He will be what we call a "frequent flyer."

Before I left, one of the other dispatchers gave me a hug and reminded me that we can't change free will, and that we should pray for the kids. Before I drift off to sleep I think of the kind of gun Dori used: a double-barreled shotgun.

I think of a six-letter word for "run rapidly."

Sprint.

Destiny, or Something

Sometimes, when people ask me how I came to be a 911 operator, I tell them it's to make sure that I'm as far away from the action as possible. You have to admit it. My end of the phone, tucked away in the dark corner of a suburban sheriff's department, is the safest place you can be some days.

I dropped out of nursing school when I was nineteen. Couldn't handle the sight of blood. And I never knew when I would get the willies or what would set me off. It didn't have to be anything big. A butterfly needle drawing blood from a patient's hand. A child crying over a gash on his knee.

One afternoon, I went on a field trip with my "Death and Dying" class to the local morgue. As the son of a son of a mortician stood in the clean, stainless-steel embalming room, explaining the process of how we *pickle* each other like cucumbers when we die, I felt all my blood fall to my feet.

Maybe it was the smell of formaldehyde, or maybe it was the glare of the sanitized scalpels, arranged on a metal sheet like cookies fresh out of the oven. When I ran out to get some air, another student followed me. He was on track for a degree in physical therapy.

"Are you okay?"

"Yeah. It's just, that *smell.*" I sat on a bench and lowered my head to ease the nausea. Learned that one in nursing school.

"Aren't you a . . ."

"Nursing student? Yeah."

"Hmm."

I've never been a huge fan of biology, either. Too many bones, muscles, and whatnot to memorize. I would glance at the pictures of various maladies and states of injury in my textbook, and I'd have to look away for fear of the head spins.

But I had this idea that I liked helping people. I came from a long line of caretakers. My gramma took care of her six brothers like they were her own children, then later took care of her alcoholic husband. My mother took care of her husband, her parents, her kids.

I had taken care of past boyfriends. I had taken care of my cat and several goldfish. I had taken care of the old folks at the nursing home where I worked in high school, my favorite job of all.

I want to take care of people.

I liked how the words sounded when they flew out of my mouth at graduation parties. I thought it made me sound noble. How can you not like a nurse? I wanted to be liked.

I like helping people.

But I didn't seem to be any good at it. Almost as strong as my desire to be a caretaker was my desire to be comfortably perfect and unchallenged. If I couldn't be a perfect nursing student, I kept thinking, then I didn't want to do it.

And then, I fell in love.

Jim was a friend of a friend. We slept together on the first date. He loved me more than I could even comprehend. It was overwhelming and mutual.

Within about a month of that date, he moved his half-full army duffel bag and his semi-warped Guild guitar into my one-bedroom apartment. I was mucking through my second round of nursing clinicals at the local veterans' hospital and failing the unit on Ace bandages when Jim spoke the most outrageous words I had ever heard.

"If you don't like it, why don't you quit?"

He was a songwriter. Not that he had ever made a dime as a songwriter, but the point is that he did what he wanted. He didn't think about how fat the paycheck would be or whether it was even feasible to make a living that way.

I had always wanted to be a nurse, but never entirely knew why. So, I made a decision. I watched a fat nurse uncap a needle with her teeth, then tell a Vietnam vet with two stumps for legs to "hold your horses," and I quit. I sold about a hundred pounds' worth of nursing textbooks back to the college, and my new love and I opened a checking account and bought a cat together. We were as good as gone.

I don't remember if my parents were disappointed. They had been through a lot with me, their only daughter, and were grateful that I was getting my life on track, paying my own rent, and staying out of trouble. But I do know that they were just a little bit concerned about the songwriter/video store sales clerk who had taken up one dresser drawer and half my soft-sided waterbed. He had long hair and wore one long earring, a cross. Yet, even to my parents, he seemed mostly harmless.

I thought about enrolling in the 911 program at the technical college; it sounded exciting. It sounded like something that would pay well, too. But I didn't follow through because mostly, I wanted to write. I was living with a man who was a slave to his creativity. I would be that way, too. Sort of.

I would be a reporter.

Now, I needed a bachelor's degree. I enrolled at the nearest private college to offer such a degree. It would have been smarter and more economical to enroll at the public university, but I had this irrational fear of parking in Minneapolis. Besides, I was getting help with my tuition from a government agency for people with disabilities. When I told my counselor at the Career Rehabilitation Center that I was switching majors, he seemed relieved. Now I wouldn't have access to narcotics anymore. He frequently asked me if nursing was the right career for me, given that I was just out of treatment for an addiction to crack cocaine.

* * *

To whoever takes this job after I leave:

I go to the Sheriff's Department every Thursday between 9 and 11 AM. They'll let you read the police reports for the week, then you can ask about anything that sticks out as being particularly newsworthy, like thefts over $500 and of course violent crimes and shootings, etc.

The clerk's name is Daria. She can be kind of a crab, but she'll give you what you need. She's been there forever.

Then if you have any questions, which you should, you go in and talk to Detective Sorenson. Sometimes they'll tell you it's "under investigation" which is code for "I'm not going to tell you anything." Sometimes you can get a little bit more if you keep at it.

Best of luck in the job. Don't let the bastards get you down.

Yours, Eric

I didn't want to take my third reporting job at the *White Bear Press*, the newspaper of White Bear Lake, my hometown and a suburb north of St. Paul. I wanted a daily paper or a magazine. The *Press* was smaller than the last one had been, and worse still, the publisher committed what I believed to be the cardinal sin of newspapers: He sold ads on the front page. Meanwhile, I worked about forty-five hours a week for what seemed like far too modest a piece of that ad revenue. Because of that, I was constantly evaluating whether or not I was "happy" in my work.

I liked being a writer, but didn't like investigating. I liked going to council meetings, but hated asking hard questions. I liked reading the police reports, but hated chasing after the brass to get the gory details. I deplored being *nosy*.

Writing opinion columns became my guilty pleasure. In columns I could rant or praise at will. I could be as wrong as I wanted to be, as long as I was *factual*. I got to write one column every other week. I could use my columns to . . . help people. Raise cancer awareness. Praise local heroes. Rip on then-governor Jesse Ventura. Whatever made me feel good.

It wasn't the *New York Times*—nor was I *New York Times* material—but it would have to do.

I had insisted that we move to White Bear Lake. Jim and I had been married about six years when we realized that we were going to become full-time parents to Jim's nine-year-old daughter, Lucy. The only mothering I had ever seen was at my parents' house on Mill Lane. The house we decided on was five minutes on foot from them, as close as we could afford to be.

Lucy had lived happily with her mom her first eight years of life, but in recent months, she had been badly neglected. She needed someone mature and grounded to fill in the holes. I was a twenty-eight-year-old nursing school dropout and an ex-addict with a writing problem.

I thought I liked helping people.

* * *

"What do I know about the job? I know that once you've been there a year, you're golden. Practically takes a letter from the governor to get you canned. You'd probably be pretty good at it. You've got a clean record and everything?"

Sergeant Sorenson of the Ramsey County Sheriff's Department probably thought he was joking, that the white-bread, big-nosed, suburban girl sitting in front of him, clutching her little reporter's notebook, should no more have a criminal record than his six-year-old grandson.

I thought it would help to get some inside scoop on this 911 thing during my weekly police report visit. It paid much better than any reporting job I'd had thus far, and if you worked more than forty hours, you got paid overtime. What a concept. And anyway, I liked helping . . . ah . . . you know. But it hadn't occurred to me that anyone would check my record, and it had been ages since I'd had to think about it. I had forgotten I had one.

"There is one thing."

"There is?"

Yeah.

"Misdemeanor? Gross-mis? Felony?" He's still in joking mode.

"Misdemeanor. I was young."

Now he's curious. "Let's run ya."

"Um, okay." Why bother saying no? He's just going to run me later if he doesn't do it right now. He's curious. Heck, I'm a little curious myself, it's been that long.

My criminal record comes back. One misdemeanor conviction for loitering and prowling in Volusia County, Florida.

As he reads it, I study the pressed wood walls of his office, a framed letter of commendation from 1985, his wife's Glamour Shots portrait on the wall. Maybe this was a bad idea.

"What were you doing in Florida?"

"Drugs."

Sorenson's eyebrows reach for the sky. "What kind of drugs?"

"Cocaine. Well, crack." I'm sweating.

"But that's not what the conviction is for, right? You didn't have anything on you, right?"

This is *so* weird. "Yeah."

Sorenson hands me the barely legible dot-matrix printout. "I wouldn't worry about it. Put your app in, anyway."

"Really?"

"Yeah. See you next Thursday."

* * *

In the space provided, please list any prior criminal history, including dates and locations. The existence of a criminal history does not automatically preclude you, the candidate, from being selected.

But let's face it, we're all cops and dispatchers here, so we're totally going to judge your ass if there is anything written here at all. But, if you don't write it, we'll still find it, and then you'll be a liar and *a criminal, so . . . there you go.*

When I met the man who introduced me to cocaine, I hated everything. I hated my brother and my parents. I hated high school.

I grew up in a devoutly Catholic family, feeling certain from a very young age that I wasn't Catholic. I had always been very shy; I lived inside my head. Every summer, my parents, my brother, and I went to my uncle's farm for a family reunion. Even in a house full of blood relatives, I could never work up the courage to talk to anyone. Instead, I would sneak out to the barn and yell "Kitty! Kitty! Kitty!" as loud as I could. The barn cats came to me. I didn't have to say the right thing. I barely had to say anything at all.

Conversely, my brother could talk endlessly without reservation, and did. At ease in almost any social setting, he was always at center stage, with children and adults alike. He was smart, bold, and fearless.

David was also hyperactive. It was a word that I learned at a very young age. Doctors tried to prescribe Ritalin, but my parents opted instead to keep us all on a no-preservative diet for many years. We could eat no food coloring, no chocolate—nothing fun. As shy as I was, I feared that this diet, meant to calm hyperactive children, would drop me right into a coma. I was reserved enough. I was quiet enough. I didn't need help. I wanted the kind of cereal that came with toys, not all-natural sugar-free granola. I wanted *chocolate.*

I hated that my brother was *hyperactive.* It was a word we used a lot; and it was *his* word, good or bad. I didn't have a word. I wasn't defined, and I didn't know how to define myself.

As my brother grew into his high school years, he became an active church group member, made a lot of friends, and found Jesus, which gave him another distinction. Two to zero. I was zero. I had no choice but to hate him.

I slunk self-consciously into my teenage years, not Catholic, not hyperactive, and still incredibly shy. The only way I could distinguish myself by then was by the things that I hated. I hated preppie kids. I hated jocks. I hated happy people. And of course, I hated religion. I wore black and smoked cigarettes. I picked friends who hated everything, too.

Despite all that, I was also haunted by the idea that what you did or didn't do in high school would absolutely shape who you became in adulthood. And if that was the case, then I would be nothing. I was about nothing and I would be nothing. Until I started getting high.

The first time I tried crack cocaine, I was someone who could barely hold three beers without barfing. I was seventeen years old and at a party with my twenty-six-year-old boyfriend, a long-haired out-of-work dry-waller named Paul. We had been introduced by a mutual friend. He liked my Farrah Fawcett hair and the way my butt looked when I wore his Levis. He didn't seem to mind that I was shy.

I turned it down at first. I didn't even know that rock cocaine was also known as crack. I had never known anyone who did it. I marveled at my new boyfriend's careful precision as he cooked the powder-and-water mixture using a metal spoon, bent at the neck. Though I had been drinking and smoking pot, I had a terrible headache and stuffy head. He told me that crack would cure my cold. I didn't believe him, but did it anyway. He was absolutely right. He was *so very right.*

After that night, I was unique. I went to school every morning knowing that I'd been higher than anyone. You can *take* your heavy-metal beer binges, all you dumb jocks, all you princesses. I get higher than you. I get so high.

I wasn't on the swim team. I didn't debate. But, I had a boyfriend who looked like a big blond god, *and I got high.*

But if I wanted to keep getting high, I had to stay with Paul. I couldn't score without him around. All the dealers who saw me wanted to "get to know me." I didn't look like a strung-out junky yet. I was thin and young, and I had all my teeth. It was too dangerous a world to wander around in without Paul. Most girls ended up giving it up for crack.

After a few months with my new loves, Paul and crack, the rest of my life began to fall away. The nursing home where I worked as a health aide fired me for failing to report to work three times in a row. The few friends I had were beginning to turn away as well. One May night, just about a week before the senior prom I never went to, four of my schoolmates showed up at the apartment I was crashing at and tried a sort of amateur intervention on me. I told them I was fine. Better than fine. Groovy. Then I went into the bathroom, got high, came back out and tried to act normal. They stopped trying after that. Even the ones who smoked cigarettes and wore black began looking at me differently.

I didn't think much about it. I was born again. Defined.

I graduated in June. My best friend kicked me out of her parents' basement. I turned eighteen in July. My mom sent a card to the house where I was staying that said, "Wherever you go, there you are."

A few days later, Paul and I left Minnesota in a brown 1986 Buick Skylark. We didn't have any special destination, but we figured we would survive by stealing, borrowing money from his relatives (mine already knew to refuse me), and selling pot.

Before I met Paul, I had barely been out of the state,

and now I was traveling all over the country like a gypsy. I thought it was exciting. We drove east to New York, then south down the coast to the Carolinas. Then we got to Florida. Stayed a little too long in Florida.

The night I was arrested, I got really lucky. If the police had caught us just a minute or so later, they might have found us with a couple rocks of cocaine. As it was, we were still waiting for it to arrive when the bicycle cop buzzed up and jammed us all up for "loitering."

I barely remember my three-day stay in the Volusia County Jail. I had been up for days; I slept the entire time. The most startling thing about being in jail was how relieved I was to be there. I couldn't hurt myself in there, and the food was free.

Paul's grandpa sent the money to bail me out; Paul picked me up in our Skylark. That night, he started to look different to me. I realized I preferred the care of Volusia County to being placed back into *his* care.

The way Paul treated other people never bothered me, because I thought I was special to him. He only looked at people he met for how they could help him. If he couldn't use someone, he would find a way to amuse himself by pushing that person's buttons. Failing that, he had no use for people at all.

After several months on the road, my use began to run out. The perky 130-pound girl with a bright smile and tight clothes slowly evolved into a 145-pound crack addict with sallow skin and stained teeth. His feelings began to change.

As had mine. Whenever I had an address long enough to receive mail, my mom sent me care packages. As the weather turned cold, she sent sweaters. Under the sweaters were pictures of my beloved cat, letters about my family, and the occasional stuffed toy.

"I saw Michelle's mom the other day," she wrote in one letter, "Michelle is assistant manager at the movie theater now, and she's started her music tech degree over in Red Wing." I put the letter down and looked around at my life. I was living in Dubuque in a cockroach-infested duplex with a drug addict. I owned a bed and a box of sweaters. She knew what she was doing.

When it ended for Paul and me, we were living in a motel room in Green Forest, Arkansas. He was getting sporadic work as a construction worker and I was working the register at a grocery store. Late one night, there was a knock at our motel room door, and Paul, half asleep, said, "Tammy, are you dressed?"

Nobody was at the door when I opened it. Paul's words hung in the air.

"Fuck," he said to his pillow.

When I asked him who Tammy was, even though I knew, he shoved me away from the bed. When I threw a shoe at him, he flew out of bed and struck me so hard across my face that my feet left the floor. When he caught up to me as I crawled toward the door, he clutched my hair tightly and screamed, "It's over!" Then he released my hair with a shove.

The next morning, he took me out to breakfast and asked if we could pretend last night never happened. *Sure*, I told him, stuffing my face with fried eggs and baking-powder biscuits, *gladly*.

After that, I couldn't stay. How could I be with someone who hit me? When he dismissed all my friends and took me away from my family, I never questioned it.

When he told me I looked like ten pounds of shit in a five-pound bag, I never saw that as abusive. But the hit was different; it was solid and real. It rested on my cheek like a boil. Every time he came near after that, I stopped breathing for a minute.

Hanging out at a pool hall the next night, Paul gestured to a sign that read: "Thanksgiving Dinner from 4 to 8 PM in the evening." I stared at it, amused at the redundancy.

"That's what we're going to do," Paul told me. "What the hell? We don't have any family, anyway, right?"

You don't, I thought. *But I do.*

The next day, when Paul went to work, I started planning my way out. I called my parents and asked them to send bus fare to the owner of the hotel, a church-going type who seemed to know without asking that I was in trouble. I thought if they sent the money directly to me, I would end up spending it on drugs.

I did all my planning behind his back. If I told him I was leaving, he would have said, *baby* and *honey* and we would have made love and tripped on acid and eaten chocolate chip cookies in bed. And then how do you leave after that?

The note on the neatly made bed of our hotel room read: *I'm sure you know where to find me, but please don't try. I'll always love you.*

I know . . . *gag me.*

It was the most natural thing in the world, leaving Paul. I don't know why I hadn't thought of it sooner. I was free. I was going to be normal again, I thought. I could get a job at another nursing home, maybe. Then

I could buy some new clothes that fit me. I could find a new boyfriend.

On the Greyhound bus to St. Paul, I sat alone for the first several hours. Then, somewhere between Joplin and Kansas City, a woman about my age plopped down in the seat across the aisle from me. She was talkative and fidgety, and her teeth were gray.

She was starting over in a new town, Des Moines, where she was going to quit "smoking" and live with a cousin. But first, one last hurrah. She was going to score in Des Moines. She knew just where because she had been there before. I told her I didn't have any money. Mostly true. That's okay, she had money. I told her I didn't want to get off in Iowa. She said, just get high and get back on the bus.

I stared at her junky eyes with my tired ones. When she took a deep breath, I heard a whistle, a sound you might expect from the lungs of a ninety-year-old on her deathbed.

"Um, no thanks," I said finally, like she had offered me a cucumber sandwich. My hand reached up to touch the hit on my cheek.

Before I met Paul, I barely knew which end of a joint was which. Now, I couldn't even get on a goddamn bus and the shit *finds me.* When the bus finally carried my rotting carcass into St. Paul, I thought of three different houses on the East Side where I knew I could score. My stomach churned in a way that only addicts know. Hungry. Ready.

I was hundreds of miles away from Paul.

Wherever you go, there you are.

I spotted my parents, rubber-necking around the bus station for me. My mom's small frame looked about ten pounds too light for her clothing. My dad held her hand and kissed the side of her head, then spoke into her ear. They both looked older, softer than I remembered. The bus doors opened and the engine sighed a long, low sigh.

I had to make a decision.

* * *

Arrested on suspicion of drug possession, pled to one misdemeanor conviction for "loitering and prowling" in Volusia County, Florida, in August 1991. Not sure on the exact date. Released after three days for time served. Volunteered for drug treatment at Anoka County Regional in December 1991 and completed 30 days successfully. I've been sober from drugs and alcohol for 10 years; I'm also a member of Alcoholics Anonymous. I'd be happy to answer any other questions in the next interview.

Assuming I get one.

* * *

When I get the call, it's not even a week after I handed in my background packet. For as much of a full cavity search as it was, it doesn't even seem like anyone looked at the darn thing. I'm almost disappointed.

My new boss, Chad Winter, invites me to spend some time with the dispatchers before I make my final decision. I schedule a visit for a balmy August Sunday afternoon.

The dispatch center is a large rectangle about the size of a living room, situated at the rear of the sheriff's department building. The security door, complete with panic bar, is propped open, and the track lighting is on, but low. There are three tall, skinny windows with teal, pleated shades pulled most of the way down and sitting crooked, as pleated shades always do. It is dusty, and the light that comes through the window reveals the particles hanging on the air.

I contemplate that. If I choose it, I will be in this room forty hours a week. Period. No leaving my desk for interviews, lunch conferences, city council meetings.

There are six work stations, and each is a cluster of three or four computer monitors, keyboards, and speakers. I can't imagine what all that is needed for. Looks like overkill, to me.

I meet Lily and Marsha, who are the most senior dispatchers of the four currently working. Marsha has been reading a paperback mystery, which she sets open and face-down on a filing cabinet. After a few minutes of pleasantries, Lily picks her book back up and begins reading again. She props her feet up on the counter of her work station. She is wearing walking sandals that show off her perfect pearl-blue pedicure.

I ask about the dress code. There is one, sort of. There used to be. Then there was a meeting about khaki pants and polo shirts, then the funding never came through for the khakis and the polos. Now it's pretty much anything goes. Excellent!

I'm there to observe the work, but for two or three hours straight, there is almost no work to observe. Marsha talks about the job for a while; she shows me how the CAD (Computer Aided Dispatch) program works. She shows me what operators see when calls come in, how the address, phone, and name pops up on a screen. But it's not always reliable, she says. *We always double-*

check. Then there are the cell phone calls, which look completely different on our computers from calls on land-lines and don't provide an address at all. Sometimes, you get a latitude and longitude reading with a callback number. Sometimes not. And never a name or an exact location.

As she talks, a 911 line lights up and I straighten, eager for something good. I pick up a secondary receiver, which lets me listen to the call while Marsha answers. But all we hear are clicks and beeps. I check the screen and see a series of numbers and letters that make no sense to me.

"Cell phone in someone's purse," Marsha sighs.

She hangs up, calls back, and admonishes the cell phone's owner.

"Your cell phone dialed 911," Marsha says, sugary. "You might want to put your key guard on. Super. *Thanks.*"

She pushes a button to disconnect.

"We're usually busier than this," she shrugs.

My training period on this job, Marsha tells me, is about three months, give or take. After that I'll be answering calls on my own. And at that point, she says, I'll know just enough to be dangerous.

Once you start answering calls on your own, and can operate either the data or fire channels well enough, then you are considered a "person." That means you're a person that Chad can put on the schedule who doesn't need a trainer listening in and telling you what to do or say. But, she says, most people say they don't really feel like they know what they're doing until they've been on the job for at least a year. *Maybe two,* someone pipes up. That seems like an exaggeration, I think.

Eventually, we stray into talk about parenting, mortgage rates, and how she's thinking about getting a Lab puppy. I have a chocolate Lab, so puppy talk swallows up almost half an hour.

We are interrupted only briefly by occasional calls on the non-emergency lines or by an officer who calls out his location on a traffic stop. Marsha says, if we get a fire call, I should go over and sit with Lisa and watch how she pages it out. But we never get a fire call. We get a medical at a nursing home. Eighty-five-year-old female with shortness of breath.

Lily dispatches it casually, then returns to her true-crime story. If I take the job, she tells me in a way that betrays nothing about her feelings on the matter, she will be my trainer. She looks back at me briefly over the pages and tells me, there is one thing. People around here can be kind of hard to work with sometimes. But you just have to remember not to take it personally. That's all. Just have a thick skin and you'll do fine.

I spend the rest of my time with them wondering if something exciting is going to happen. It doesn't. I figure, *This looks easy enough.*

* * *

Giving my notice at the newspaper is effortless. I have been there exactly one year, which is about as long as I've stayed at any job. I get restless. I start complaining. Then I move on to what I always assume are wildly greener pastures.

Ramsey County, I believe, is where I'll finally be happy.

* * *

My first few days are a cakewalk. Marlys is the first of my three trainers. During my month with her, I work day shift. Day shift is by far the most desired shift, generally gobbled up by the dispatchers with the most seniority.

Marlys has been a dispatcher for at least three sheriffs' terms. She is soft-spoken and patient. She feeds me the job in tiny little bites. She shows me how to "key the mike" before I use it to talk on the fire department radio. (Pause, push the transmit button, then talk.) She lets me pick up only the non-emergency lines when they ring. She lets me sit back and listen in when she takes the tough calls: medicals and domestics and such. She tells me not to rush into things. For now, she tells me, I will just learn how to operate on the fire channel and the data channel. The fire channel is for dispatching firefighters. The data channel is for helping officers by running driver's license checks on traffic stops, for example.

The main channel, I quickly learn, is the *thing*. The main channel is not for the meek. The main is the operator who dispatches the officers to the calls we get. The main answers officers' calls for help. The main has to know what everyone is doing at all times, where they're doing it, and with how much backup. The main has to stay calm when everyone else is frantic. When the shit hits the fan, it hits the main the hardest. The dispatcher on the main has to be a control freak to do it right, and he or she must control from miles away, with nothing but a microphone.

A language other than English is spoken on the main channel. Officers are called by a number, like 2585 or 2453, not a name.

"2585, what's your location?"

Some departments speak only in 10-codes.

Dispatcher: "2585, are you 10-8 (in service)?"

Squad 2585: "Affirmative."

Depending on the tone of voice used, that's code for "Can you put the apple fritter down and take a call now? Your shift started half an hour ago." And from 2585: "Yes, mother."

And each exchange ends not with an "over and out" like you might see in the movies, but a marking of the time.

"2585, what's your status?"

"2585, I'm Code 4."

"Copy . . . Code 4 at 20:52."

Translated: "2585, everything okay?"

2585: "Yes, Mother."

Dispatch: "Super! You're okay and it's 8:52 PM."

I imagine that once you've spoken this language for a few months, it becomes increasingly difficult to navigate a fast-food drive-through without making a fool out of yourself.

"Your total is $3.43, please pull ahead to the second window."

"Copy, 12:35."

"Pardon me?"

"Uh, thanks."

Perhaps the reason for all the 10-codes and fancy talk is to throw off people who listen to police scanners, like news reporters and Nosy Nellies. But unless you're a seasoned veteran, it's hard to conceal the sense of panic you feel when you ask an officer if he or she is Code 4 and you hear "*NEGATIVE!*" Now, without letting on that you're shitting yourself, you must calmly announce to the other officers on the main that your guy needs help. Then you have to sit there and hope he gets it in time.

I learn new ways to say words which I didn't realize needed to be modified, such as D-K for "drunk" and GOA and DOA for "gone" and "dead," respectively. Negative and affirmative, for "no" and "yes."

I learn the codes that we use to "close" the calls the cops go on.

For example: Officer 2460: "2460, clear me Code 20."

Dispatch: "Copied. Clear at 14:55."

That means 2460 is done with that call and ready for the next one. For the purposes of record-keeping, the dispatcher enters the code into the CAD system, then the call is officially police history.

The codes give us only small clues about how these calls end. Code 20 means the call was cleared with no report. Police took nobody to detox, witnessed no crimes, got into no fights, made no arrests, secured the peace, and got the heck outta there. Code 1 means a report. Any number of things may have happened. Maybe somebody got arrested. Maybe somebody got cited for DWI. Maybe a child went into foster care. Any kind of theft requires a report, no matter how big or small. Like everything else, all these rules can differ from one department to another. Some departments require their cops to write reports on every call, no matter what happened. Even if everybody's GOA.

When dispatchers broadcast suspect information on the main, they had better do it in the proper order. The first qualifier is always race: Asian, white, black, unknown. Then it's sex: male, female, unknown. Then approximate age, then descriptors, starting from the top down. Hair color and length, eyes, shirt, pants, shoes.

"All squads, your suspect is a white male in his thirties with short blond hair, blue eyes, a black Beavis and Butt-Head T-shirt, holey jeans, and purple Converse high tops."

The best way to sound like a plebe on the main is to get it all backwards.

"All squads, your suspect is wearing purple tennies, and he's a white guy with blue hair and blond eyes."

Along with the language of the main channel is the protocol. Since the main channel is monitored by so many people—neighboring departments, higher-ups, news media, Joe and Lena Johnson in their kitchen—it's important to always be professional. It's important not to make a jerk out of yourself, even when tested, Marlys warns. It could wind up on the evening news, or worse, in a courtroom.

"2453, are you clear to take a domestic in the township?"

"Negative, I checked out of service ten minutes ago," complete with sarcastic edge.

Key mike: "Copy, 10:45." Un-key mike. "What am I, his secretary now?" Every once in a while, the mike gets stuck and a dispatcher ends up making an apology for saying something meant to be off the air.

It is rare that a dispatcher lets loose on the main.

Marlys tells me about one incident, which everyone seems to know about, in which Lily talked back to a deputy on the main. She was sending him to a fight involving at least five males; a dispatcher would always send at least two cops for that, maybe three. He answered back that he would "advise" on the call, meaning that he would go alone, without backup.

Advising is something cops apparently do a lot of that they shouldn't. Sometimes they do it because they know everyone else is busy, but sometimes they do it out of machismo. 2453 had advised in similar situations, and Lily wasn't in the mood for an "officer down" kind of afternoon, so she gently prodded.

"2453, we're told there are more than five males involved in this fight."

"Copied. I'll advise."

2453 is about 5 feet 9, 175.

Pause. Mike keyed . . .

"*You'll advise until you get your ass kicked, then you won't advise anymore.*" For all the world to hear. " . . . 17:58."

Guess she didn't want him to get his ass kicked.

At this point, I can't even imagine dispatching on the main, let alone lipping off to a cop on the main. But I won't have to worry about that with Marlys. Marlys prefers the data channel. She likes it so much, she comes in twenty minutes early every day just to make sure nobody else gets it. Maybe that's why she's so laid back. She doesn't work the main and doesn't have to.

* * *

"2460?"

"2460."

"Sending you to . . . standby one . . . sending you to 3000 Wells Drive on a theft from vehicle report."

"Copy . . . is 2462 on the board?"

Shit. That's not his area.

"Sorry . . . 2462?"

"2462."

"Sending you the call I just sent 2460."

"You're going to have to repeat it."

I would love to, but I just pushed a button that erased the damned thing from my screen.

"Copy, um, 3000 Wells Drive . . . standby one . . ."

Lily reaches around me, keys the mike and says over my shoulder, "6-0 you can disregard Wells Drive and 6-2, it's 3000 Wells Drive on a theft from auto. Meet your comp at the front entrance."

"Copy."

"18:38."

It's been almost three hours of this. Three hours of me hopelessly botching the simplest of tasks on the main channel, for all the world to hear.

It doesn't matter to me that I'm not going to be expected to handle the main for at least another four or five months, and even then, it will be as a back-up person. I want easy. I want to be a natural. I want this to be my calling.

It's my fifth week on the job. So far, in my career at Ramsey County, I've transferred three different callers to the wrong ambulance services, I've taken I-don't-know-how-many calls that turned out not to be in our jurisdiction, and I've gained three pounds. Okay, seven.

The first four weeks of gentle prodding and patient explanation with Marlys have ended. I am in the "sink or swim" phase of training.

I can't believe all the shit they're trying to cram into my head. It's not human. There are at least six different channels buzzing with traffic all night and I can never figure out when they're talking to *me*. I paged out the wrong fire department to a fire alarm last week. I sent animal control to an address that didn't exist. When a woman called because her child had been hit by a car, my first thought was: *She should call 911. Oh my God, I AM 911.*

Since they stuck me on afternoon shift with Lily, I haven't seen my husband or my stepdaughter in three days, and I'll be on this shift for a whole month. The house is a mess. I'm tired all the time. I've developed my first pimple in four years. Dead center of my forehead.

Now I'm going to go cry like a big baby.

"I'm going to the bathroom," I say under my breath.

I sit on the toilet and bawl. I've never sucked this bad at anything, and that's saying something. Somebody's going to die because of me, I'm certain. Why did they hire me? Didn't they see my checkered past? I'm a criminal who spent two nights in jail! This is such a joke. I don't know what I was thinking.

It's clear that my coworkers have no idea that I'm a former crack addict, but in fact, it's my status as a former reporter that makes people nervous. One day, a deputy jokes in a dry tone that I may be a plant from the newspaper, working on some kind of tell-all exposé on the sheriff's department. If only that were true, I think. If only I were just biding my time until I finish my twelve-part series on what it's like to be a 911 phone-jockey. Alas, it is not so. I am just a girl with a simple goal: to earn a paycheck and to not kill anybody today.

After a few minutes, Lily finds me rinsing my red face in the sink.

"What's going on?"

"I just don't know if I belong here."

"You belong here. You're fine. We all go through this."

"Everything else I've ever done, I've been good at. I mean, I don't aim all that high . . . but, like, every other job I've ever had, I've been good at long before this."

"Well, this isn't like a lot of jobs. And, by the way, you can't just run out of the room."

Not even if you're having a hissy fit?

"Oh . . . sorry."

If Lily has ever shed a tear in this bathroom, you couldn't tell by looking at her. She stands in front of me like a sentry, arms crossed. She has no interest in this little pity party I'm throwing.

"You're smart enough to do this." Lily pauses; maybe she's seeing if she's got my attention. "And once you get it, you'll know that you can just about do anything. Maybe that's why you need to be here."

I feel like a little kid. We hug.

"Okay."

"Okay. Ready?"

"Ready."

* * *

Entering the comm center at shift change one Friday night, I can tell I'm in the middle of a situation. Scotty, a former postman with a young face and gray hair, is standing at his console with an anxious look. He is wearing a headset and his yellow phone light is on, meaning he's talking to someone.

Kristen nods to him, and then he says, to whomever is at the other end: "Sir, you have to put the gun on the floor, then go to the front door with your hands up. If you do that, you won't get hurt."

I'm agog. We get to say stuff like that? Awesome.

Scotty goes on: "Sir, you have to show them you don't have a gun, then. You have to go to the door with your hands up. Yep. Okay. Go do that."

I'm so stoked. I can't wait until the day I get to tell someone to put his hands in the air, just like Cagney and Lacey, but tucked safely out of danger, ten miles away from the scene.

* * *

One of the best things about being in training is hearing other dispatchers' stories of failure. They see you messing up right and left and it inspires them to share, I guess.

One of my favorites came from Marsha. A 911 call came in from a factory I'll call Technology, Inc., and although the company had several locations in the metro area, there was only one in our jurisdiction. The caller told Marsha that someone had been severely burned with some kind of acid. The caller was extremely agitated, as anyone would be. Marsha got police and medics going, but in the hysteria, she never actually confirmed the address with the caller.

A few minutes later, Marsha's caller was back on the line, demanding to know where the medics were. The victim was in excruciating pain.

Marsha checked with her officers on the main channel, then got back on the phone and told her caller, "The officers are just entering off Highway 10; they'll be there in just one minute."

"Highway 10?" the caller said. "We're in Minneapolis, you dumb bitch!"

Marsha didn't know until that moment that Technology Inc.'s phone system had caused the call from Minneapolis to be routed to the company's main switchboard in our county. She never made *that* mistake again.

Marlys told me about the first medical she ever took. An elderly woman called and said she thought her husband was having a heart attack. Overwhelmed, Marlys started to cry.

And everyone seemed to have an "Oops, I forgot to send the ambulance" story.

Still, training felt like a sort of boot camp to me. I felt like everyone was waiting for me to screw up so they could yell me back into line. And there were *so many* varied and interesting ways to screw up because there was *so damn much* to know.

Ramsey County operators dispatch for a total of ten different cities within the county. Of those, Mounds View, Roseville, and New Brighton have their own police departments. White Bear Township, Little Canada, Shoreview, Arden Hills, Gem Lake, and North Oaks do not have their own departments, and therefore contract with Ramsey County to be patrolled by Ramsey County deputies. We also dispatch to the St. Anthony officers who patrol Lauderdale and Falcon Heights, two teensy little towns on the border of St. Paul.

And, breathe.

We dispatch for the Falcon Heights Fire Department, the Little Canada Fire Department, the Lake Johanna Fire Department (which puts out fires in Shoreview, Arden Hills, and North Oaks), and the Vadnais Heights Fire Department. White Bear Township and Gem Lake use the White Bear Lake Fire Department. But we don't dispatch to the White Bear Lake Fire Department; they have their own dispatch. But we do send our deputies to their fires. But only in cases of a big-deal type of fire. The small-deal types of fires get handled by a fire officer. Got it?

I'm not done yet.

Different cities are served by different ambulance services. White Bear Township and Gem Lake use White Bear Lake Fire, for whom we don't dispatch (see above). Mounds View, Roseville, New Brighton, Shoreview, Little Canada, Arden Hills, and North Oaks contract with a private ambulance service, and Falcon Heights and Lauderdale use St. Paul Medical, dispatched out of St. Paul.

And all the this information must be burned on your brain, so you can remember what to do while someone's screaming in your ear. And so you don't send the wrong cop or the wrong firefighter to the wrong thing and get everybody all excited over nothing.

And I'm not done. Never done.

Mounds View and New Brighton officers send their officers to help people who are locked out of their cars. St. Anthony will do lockouts, but only if the car has manual locks. Roseville and the others won't do them unless there's a child locked in the car. Dogs don't count as children, as it turns out. Who knew?

And it's not just lockouts. Each of the different patrolling agencies has different policies about everything you can think of, like how many officers can go on lunch break at the same time or how many cars get sent to this or that call, or whether we'll even send help to someone who's got a bat in a bedroom or a raccoon in a window well, or if that person has to call someone else, like pest control or something. And then someone complains about a policy and the policy changes again.

And don't forget: Don't talk to the media. Sometimes they're just cold-calling to see what they can find. Sometimes they are following up on some half-assed tip. Either way, tell them nothing's going on. If there's actually some big dang deal going on and you can't deny it, then get a phone number and page a sergeant.

Never leave the room with fewer than three operators, and don't leave the building unless the supervisor approved it. Don't pop your microwave popcorn inside the comm center. The smell pisses everybody off. And whatever you do, don't burn it. That'll piss everybody off from the dispatch center down to the squad room.

* * *

After each shift, I sit blindly in front of the TV, the ring of the 911 phones in my ears. Sometimes the phone rings at home for me, but I would rather die than spend another minute talking on the phone. I've lost the ability to *chat.*

Sometimes I dream about calls I took earlier that day, but in my dreams, I forget to send anyone, then an hour or more passes and I'm doing my nails or reading the paper and someone says, "Did you remember to dispatch that call?" Or maybe I forget to check a cop's status on a traffic stop and when I finally call out to check on him or her, I get no answer. No answer. Then someone gets hurt. Then I get yelled at. Stupid stupid stupid.

I dream I am punching lines and I can hear my callers, but they can't hear me, so they start to panic, thinking nobody is coming to help. When I try to yell to them, nothing comes out. Then I realize my headset's not plugged in; I can't seem to fix it. And there's nobody around to help me.

Sometimes, I dream I am at work, then look down and realize I am wearing nothing but my head set. Okay, everybody gets that one. Don't they?

When people ask me what I do for a living, I avoid the question. I'm not yet what I am trying to be. It feels disrespectful to real 911 operators for me to go around saying that I am one of them.

* * *

Part of my training is learning to dispatch to firefighters and medics on the "fire channel." To the untrained ear, radio chatter sounds pretty simple. But as with everything else in this job, there's a right way, and there are a hundred wrong ways. My first few transmissions over the fire channel are a demo tape of most of the wrong ways. I'm too slow. I'm too fast. I'm too loud. I'm too quiet. I'm too wordy. I'm too unspecific. Ooh, and my favorite thing to do is called *uptalking*.

Uptalking is when you make a statement, but end with an upward lilt, as if you're asking a question? But if you say it like a question and it isn't, you risk not being understood? Then there's the fact that you sound like a newbie moron.

The first time I dispatch a fire call, I blurt out, "Check for a smell of smoke on the third floor of 120 Destiny Road?" Should they or shouldn't they check for a smell of smoke? Heaven only knows.

When my first firefighter checks in on the air, he speaks slowly, as if he knows that he's dealing with a newbie moron. "Lake Johanna . . . Chief 14 . . . en route, Ramsey."

This is where I have to do two things. I have to tell the computer that he's en route to the call, and I have to respond on the air to Chief 14. I send both messages to my brain, but they run into each other *en route,* get into a fist fight, which causes an explosion in my cerebral cortex, and what happens next is:

"Copy . . . Chief 4 . . . 18:45."

And I type:

"Chief 10 en route."

* * *

Once my three months of training are done, and I am considered a "person," I go to the shift that isn't a shift at all: vacation relief.

Vacation relief is a relief to everybody except the dispatcher who has to work it. It is a way to fill holes in the schedule, and it generally goes to the lowest man (or woman) on the seniority totem pole. On vacation relief, I might work three afternoon shifts in a row, then a day shift, then a day or two off, then night shifts for a week. Or maybe I work night shift one day, then day shift for the next three. My circadian rhythm doesn't know whether it's on foot or horseback. I live month to month, waiting eagerly for the schedule to come out, to see if the wheel has spun in my favor or not.

Physically, I'm a mess. I'm gaining weight from trying to eat away the stress of chaos followed by boredom. After a few months, the vending machine supplier notices a spike in sales and starts stocking two rows' worth of chocolate Zingers, seemingly just for me. I become a connoisseur of pizza, sesame chicken, hoagies, and anything else that can be brought by a delivery driver. (In general, it's better to have food delivered than to send a dispatcher out to get it, just in case the shit hits the fan.)

The cold that visited me in my first week on the job returns four times before I finally get rid of it. My coworkers observe my coughing and sniffling from a distance, then nervously sanitize their own phones and keyboards, just in case. I don't want to show up to work sick, yet I notice that when others use their sick time, it is immediately assumed that they aren't really sick.

I am given an alpha pager, which sends me text messages asking for overtime volunteers for various shifts when others call in sick, which happens all the time. But I am away from Jim and Lucy so often, and at such odd hours, that all I can do is set the pager to "vibrate" when I'm home and pretend I don't hear it.

I just want to get by. I want to get to that magical time when I know what the hell I am doing. Some say it takes a year, some say longer. I want to be a good dispatcher. I want to save lives, but I'm willing to settle for just *not killing anybody*.

For once, I want to learn how to get good at something I seem to be supremely bad at. I want to live outside the comfort of being a mediocre journalist, a mediocre wife and mother, a mediocre person. I know that if I get past a certain point, that I can say I'm a part of something important. Lily says that I belong here, and that there is a reason I'm supposed to be here.

I want that to be true.

On-the-Job Training

"911?"

"We just got robbed."

"With a gun?"

Marlys had told me that when people say they've been "robbed," most of the time they really mean that someone broke into their car or something. You ask, "With a gun?" so you know exactly what you're dealing with right away. The answer is almost never "yes."

"Yes."

"You were robbed with a gun?"

"Yes!"

"Uh, armed robbery," I yell over my half-wall to the lead dispatcher, Kristen.

"Well, put it in," she says matter-of-factly. She can't

dispatch it until I label the call and drop the address into our computer system, which of course still takes me longer than anyone else in the room. I transmit the call, but I have attached the wrong type-code to it, so instead of labeling it as "armed robbery, hot" or ARH, I have labeled it as "accident, hit and run" or "AHR."

Once again, I've taken time out of my busy work day to be a complete idiot. Thank God for my partner, Lisa, who changes it from her computer faster than I can say . . .

"So, you're at the Mini Mart?"

"Yes." My caller might be in shock. That makes two of us.

"What's your name?" I'm trying to get the info in the order of the little blanks on my screen.

Kristen stands up and stares at me. I can tell she would prefer that *anyone* but me had taken this call. I'm still too slow and mechanical. "Suspect information?" she says impatiently. "Car? Weapon? Direction of travel?"

By the time I get everything we need to know from my caller, our suspects have likely driven eighty miles to Rochester and are ordering their second round of martinis at the St. James Hotel, but I try not to let that bother me. When I do, I move even slower.

My caller tells me he was pistol-whipped during the robbery. This makes my heart race. *He needs you to be the calm one,* I tell myself. *He's been through enough.*

When the cops get there and it's time for us to disconnect, I tell the clerk he did a good job. I heard Lily say that to a caller once. Then I sit back and tell myself the same thing. I did it. I took my first hot call. I resisted the urge to crawl into a ball under the console and cry for my mommy. Instead, I did the job. I didn't do it perfectly. But I didn't suck, and I didn't kill anybody.

I'm buzzed.

The robbers are GOA.

Kristen stands up and turns to me. She has been on the job more than thirty years. Tonight, she is the shift supervisor; she is the main. All calls go through her.

Kristen is dark and Romanian, short and pear-shaped, with a prominent nose and piercing eyes. Her voice is low and even, and she can dispatch a double murder with the same calm demeanor of anyone else dispatching a vandalism-to-mailbox call. She hates incompetence, and she is never wrong. She is not a trainer by choice, but her seniority often puts her on the spot to be one. She scares the living shit out of me.

We are separated by a set of cubicle partitions which are about half the height of most cubicles. Perhaps the room is designed that way so that we can see to talk to one another, but we can't physically reach over and strangle each other.

She is about to critique my performance, and I know it. This has become the routine. She will not wait for a moment when we can be alone. And anyway, we can't both leave the room.

"Caroline, you need to talk to *me* when you're taking those calls. You need to ask them what I ask you when I ask you. I'm the one who needs to know."

I feel my face getting hot. I'm getting a performance review in front of a room full of people. "Okay," I say lamely.

"I can't read your mind. You need to speak up."

"I thought I *was* answering your questions," I say stupidly.

"Well, trust me, you weren't."

"Okay."

"Okay, then." Her eyebrows are up. She is imparting something. There is something I'm supposed to *get*. And she doesn't want to have to tell me again.

She leaves the room to go smoke a cigarette, which she does several times a shift. This job makes me want to smoke. Smoking appears to be the only acceptable reason to walk away during the course of a shift. Eating can be done while answering the phones.

Kendra, who is about two years new on the job, waits for the door to close behind Kristen before she says, "You did fine. That's just Kristen. Don't take it personally."

* * *

The first time I realize that people lie to the police—I mean people lie *big*—is during a domestic argument call. I am still in training with Lily, and my caller, a younger man, tells me he's been fighting with his girlfriend. I am trained to ask if there are any weapons involved, so I do.

He pauses, then says, "Yeah, uh. She has a .32. I mean a .22. She got a .22."

A gun? Oh my God!

"You mean she's got a gun right now, James?"

I say it loud enough for the whole room to hear, so someone can call the officers over the main and alert them to imminent danger. Danger, Will Robinson!

"Yeah. And she punched me, too."

Lily has been listening quietly on an extension, but

she has had about had enough of the James Jackson Story Hour, so she takes over the call from there.

The truth is, there was no gun, no punch, and after all that, there was probably no girlfriend anymore either. Actually, there had been one punch, but James had been the puncher. If everyone involved with that call had been as gullible as I, his poor girlfriend might have even been cuffed and stuffed, bloody nose and all.

I had no idea. Even when I had been in trouble with police, I would never have lied. That's illegal or something, right?

I had been a sucker.

I wouldn't let that happen again. From then on, I wouldn't believe every little thing a caller told me. I would be skeptical, critical. This job was going to give me a skin. I wasn't going to be that bright-eyed and naïve girl from the suburbs anymore.

A few weeks later, and away from the safety net of Lily's training, I take a call from a lady I'll call Linda. Linda tells me she was raped by her husband, well, her ex-husband, she says. She seems to be choosing her words one at a time. She is nervous. Armed with my new-found no-shit attitude, I decide she is probably lying.

They had gone out and gotten drunk, she tells me. This only cements what I think I already know about her, about her life and the choices she makes. I even remember that I have sent squads to her house before, for other things.

I interrupt her to get her name, number, and the address where the incident occurred. We are filling out a form. I keep an even, cold demeanor. I don't believe her;

I refuse to get sucked in. I'm just going to get the info and send the squads, who won't believe her either.

She continues. They had gone out, gotten drunk, and he had forced himself on her. She says carefully, "He held me down and raped me."

From somewhere within the range of her telephone, I hear him coming toward her and talking. I hear him say that she's full of shit, and that she should get off the phone. "Nobody will believe you," he tells her.

Nobody believes her.

"You raped me," she says, crying now. "*Get away from me.*"

When she says it, I am hit with something. I'm eighteen, living with Paul, a thousand miles from home. I am that girl he hit one night. After that, every time he comes near me, I tighten. I can't wait to get away.

She is that girl as well. I can tell it like I can tell you the color of my hair or the day I was born.

When he takes the phone from her, I hear the fear in her sobbing. He is drunk, and he wants me to know his side of the story. I won't get to talk to her again.

As he rambles, I get two squads going to their place, and I send an ambulance to stand by for her. I don't want to hear his side, and the second the squads arrive, I disconnect without a goodbye.

He raped her. And I helped.

Of course, I sent all the people I needed to send, but a trained monkey can do that. I had been indifferent. I had been matter-of-fact and cool, because I wasn't going to let her make a fool of me if she was lying. I had not given comfort; I hadn't given anything. And it was too late to undo the damage from what I had not done.

That day changed the rules for me again.

After that day, I had one rule: That I don't know *anything*, and because of that, I didn't want to pretend that I did with another single human being, ever.

* * *

I am midway through a busy afternoon shift when I get a medical call from a woman whose husband is having a heart attack. She tells me he weighs somewhere between 400 and 450 pounds. When the officers arrive, we get the update on the main channel. 2460 says simply: "Full arrest."

"Full arrest" almost always means death, or "DOA" as the cops always say. Sure, defibrillators look really cool on TV. The TV doctor yells "Clear!" then he shocks the patient back to life and everyone sighs with relief. That scene is very rare in the real world.

The officers are on scene with this medical for much longer than usual, since the medics have decided to keep working on him at the scene. He must be too heavy to transport, someone in the comm center remarks. Then one of the officers calls the comm center on his cell phone. He tells me to page the on-duty chaplain.

Chaplain Bill Hislop, captain of the God Squad (the Chaplain Corps), is one of my favorite people because he's nice to me. Perhaps it's because he's not around enough to know what a plebe I am. I've likely interrupted his dinner, given the time of day, but he doesn't say a word about that, just asks for a moment to grab a pen. I slowly recite to him the address of the medical, where he will go for as long as he is needed for absolutely no pay and give comfort to the family of the deceased.

But before I disconnect with him, I hear something I didn't expect. "They got him back," Marsha informs me. By the tone of her voice, I can tell that doesn't happen much.

"Got who back? What? On Murphy Street?"

"Yep. They're taking him to the hospital. You can cancel Bill."

"Awesome."

The rest of the room appears oblivious. But I took the call. I sent people and they saved him. Marsha gives me a wink. She's happy for me, but too busy to get all excited.

The phones keep ringing, so all I have time to do is grin like a goofball for the rest of the shift. I can't help myself. I did what I could do . . . and the heart of someone I will never meet is beating again.

* * *

"911?"

"I want someone to come arrest my mom. She's doing drugs."

"She's doing drugs right now?"

"Yeah, she locked herself in the bathroom and she's smoking crack. She does it all the time."

"What's your name?"

"Darius."

"Darius, how old are you?"

"Fourteen."

"Okay, we have a couple squads on the way, but I want you to stay on the phone with me so I know you're okay 'til they get there."

"Okay."

"Does she have any weapons?"

"No. . . . *Mom, I told you I's going to call! I don't want you to get high anymore!*"

"Is she mad at you for calling?"

"Yeah. But I'm tired of this stuff."

"Of course you are. You're very brave for calling."

"Well, thanks. I guess."

"Is she still in the bathroom?"

"Yeah."

"Is she going to fight the cops, do you think?"

"I don't know. She's all different when she's smoking crack. Are they going to hurt her?"

I've been trained never to make promises on behalf of the officers. If she fights, they might throw her on the floor, kneel on her back, and cuff her. Is it going to hurt? Probably. I hope she doesn't fight. If she gets hurt, will Darius ever call us again, even if he needs us?

"I don't think so, Darius." It's complicated, I want to tell him.

What follows is a long, awkward pause. I've run out of questions and the cops aren't there yet. I look to my computer screen, to my half-lost game of digital solitaire. I use my mouse to move the jack of hearts onto the queen of clubs. I noticed Lily one night, playing computer games while talking to a suicidal. At the time, I thought it strange. But I'm beginning to see why she did it. It takes the pressure off. I'm not in that house, I'm here playing solitaire.

"What grade are you in, Darius?"

"Eighth."

"What's your favorite subject?"

"Lunch."

Shit. I'm asking questions that require only one word answers, so that's all I'm getting. I place the ace of spades at the top of my screen, then "reshuffle" the cards.

"How long has your mom been in the bathroom?"

"She ran in there when I got home from school. . . . Hang on . . . the cops are here."

I wish I could hug the kid. He trusted me with his mom.

"Okay, kiddo. You did good. Goodbye."

The officers clear the call a Code 20—no report—in the time it takes me to finish my game.

* * *

"911?"

"I'm not feeling too good."

"What's wrong?"

"I don't want to live."

"Where are you?"

"No . . . I don't want to live, that's all."

"Maybe we can help."

"I doubt it."

"Can I send someone to talk you about what's wrong?"

"I don't want anyone."

"What's your name?"

"Sandy."

"What's your last name?"

"No, I don't want that."

"What do you mean?"

"I mean don't ask me that."

"Sandy, why do you want to hurt yourself?"

Oh shit. She didn't say that, she said she didn't want to

live. Shit shit. Get yourself off automatic pilot. Listen. Listen to her.

"I don't . . . I don't know."

Did I plant an idea?

"Have you been drinking?"

"A couple beers."

"I wish you'd tell me where you are, Sandy. I want to help you."

"I can't. I don't . . . I can't."

We go round and round and round for about half an hour. She lives with a man named Kenny. Her family doesn't understand her. She is drinking Budweiser in the can and she wants to find a job where they don't treat her like a mule.

I feel such a responsibility for the Sandys of the world. I never want to let any of them down. I let her talk. When she's had enough of my stupid questions, she hangs up. We never found her. I hope I helped.

* * *

"911?"

"Hi. My name is Amber Gillis. My husband was using a table saw and cut two of his fingers off."

"What, he cut his fingers off?"

"Yeah. Could you send an ambulance?"

"He just did this now?"

"Yeah. Just now."

"Uh, of course! Yes. What's your address?"

"4555 Blue Jay Avenue. Best way to get here is to take . . ."

"Just one second, ma'am! Is he conscious and breathing?"

"Oh, sure. Yeah. And we've got the fingers right here."

"Uh, okay. Uh, hold on and I'll transfer you to the ambulance service for pre-arrival."

"Okay."

I transfer the line, disconnect, then look down at my hands.

"You would *not* believe how calm that woman was," I say to nobody in particular. I take a look at my own hands, still intact, shaking.

* * *

"911?"

"Send someone to Douglas Street!"

"What?"

"Douglas Street! Hurry!"

"Where on Douglas Street?"

"Dog bite!"

"What's wrong?"

"Dog bite! Dog bit him! Oh God."

"Who?"

"This is Renee."

"*Oh.*"

Renee is one of our cops. While off duty, she has seen a dog attack a man. The wound goes straight to the victim's bone, like something out of the movie *Jaws*.

"Wow, you wouldn't believe how hysterical Renee was," I say to the room at large, when things quiet back down. To tell the truth, I am relieved to see that I'm not the only who flips out around here.

* * *

"911?"

"Yeah, we want to make a report for our son. He says he was molested by a guy from our church, and the guy has admitted to it already."

"How old is your son?"

"He's six."

"Does the suspect know you're calling police?"

"Yes, he's here with us."

"With you right now?"

"Yes."

"Is he under control?"

"Yes, he's fine. He's going to cooperate with you guys. It's fine."

The guy is a drifter, sixty-seven years old. We run his criminal history for the officer who starts the investigation. He has seven prior arrests and convictions for molesting children in all different parts of the country.

Lily uses the printout as a training tool, showing me how to read the heavily coded cop-speak, even though we are officially past training. She shows me how to tell whether his various crimes were felonies or misdemeanors, when he was convicted, where he did his time, and the rest of it. To my relief, she does not try to hide that she, like me, is repulsed by what we are reading.

"Penetration" is the word used to say that he has had sex with boys. "Contributing to the delinquency of" means that he gave them drugs or alcohol. "Failure to comply" means he never went to his court-ordered sex-offender treatment. Some of his victims are adults now. For each one on our printout, there could be dozens more who never reported him.

Now, he is older, still unable to resist his impulses,

and almost begging to be thrown back into prison. Maybe it's the only way he knows how to be saved from his inability to keep from hurting children. Maybe he needs the roof over his head.

I check the clock and see that it's 8:35 PM, time enough before bedtime. I call home and say goodnight to Lucy, who I pray to God would tell us if anyone *ever* hurt her.

* * *

Just a few months into the job, I learn to dislike reporters. It matters not that I recently was one of them. That seems a million miles away. And if I didn't like the "scoop" mentality before, now I detest it.

They call at all different hours of the day and night to ask if anything is going on that they should know about. They say they're "just checking in," and they call on the non-emergency lines, not the 911 lines. Doesn't matter. Still bugs me. When I was a reporter, I never called a 911 dispatcher just to "check in." But, I also never worked for a daily newspaper or a major TV station. Or, God forbid, Fox News.

When they're not busy cold-calling for news stories, they're listening to the scanners for anything that sounds bloody. Car crashes, chases, violent domestics, armed robberies, and whatnot. They hear only snippets of what's going on, such as a dispatcher relaying something about a Hispanic male walking down the street with a rifle, then they call us while we're in the middle of trying to find out if there really is a Hispanic male walking down the street with a rifle, and they say things like: "We understand there's been a shooting. What can you tell us about it?"

One day, I get a call from the reporter at the *White Bear Press* who had the grievous misfortune of replacing me. "Caroline? This is Natalie! Remember me? I worked with you at the *Press*?"

"Mmmhmm. Sure." I immediately recognize the over-friendly tone she's taking with me; it's the singsongy lilt of a reporter under deadline.

"Well, I'm just calling because I'm curious about something."

"Mmmhmm?"

When addressing the media, I like to keep my lips as close together as possible, as if enunciating will somehow let out too many revealing syllables in the process. The truth is, it's ridiculous for reporters to ask us anything; we have no authority to give out information and they know it.

"There's, like, a whole bunch of county squad cars outside the funeral home downtown here, and I'm curious what's that about?"

"Hold on."

The squad cars are there for a funeral. The daughter of one of our lieutenants has died of after a protracted illness. She was young, and it is sad. But I know it's nothing the newspaper would ever report on. After getting Marsha's advice on what to say, I get back on the phone with Natalie.

"One of our deputies lost a daughter. It's not a murder or anything like that. The deputies are there to show their support."

She pauses, then thanks me and hangs up.

Two minutes later, she is on the phone again. She's

still got her friendly reporter voice on, but it's starting to fray a little. "Eleanor wanted me to call you back," she says, slickly deflecting the responsibility for what she's about to ask. "She wants to know how she died."

* * *

We keep a list of anyone who calls us to say that they've either lost a pet or found one, along with a description of the delinquent critter. It's called the "pet board."

One evening I get a call from a guy saying he's found a big fat gray cat dead on the side of the road in Shoreview. I check the pet board, and sure enough, there's a Mrs. Darlene Johnson who's been looking for her gray cat since yesterday. Mrs. Johnson lives in the same neighborhood as deadgraycatonthesideoftheroad.

Crap.

I have three cats, and I know the sudden death of any one of them would absolutely ruin me. They're my furry little children. I also know that if my cat were deadonthesideoftheroad, I would want to know right away and not have to wonder.

So I hem and haw and sweat a little, and think of what words to say to poor Mrs. Johnson. I imagine Mrs. Johnson lives alone with little (big) Fluffy or Muffy or Bitsy and just *lives* for her dear old cat, judging by its portly nature and by the way she called police on the first day it went on walkabout. I even consider calling the on-duty chaplain, then think better of it. Around here, that's the kind of thing that'll keep cops and dispatchers ripping on you for months.

When Mrs. Johnson picks up the phone, I go straight into what I like to think is a very soothing tone of voice, reserved for the gravest of situations, as this is. "I'm so sorry to have to tell you this," I say, "but I think we found your cat . . . and . . . well, it's been hit by a car. It's dead. Deadonthesideoftheroad. I'm so sorry!"

I'm almost in tears until, not even one bit shocked or distressed, Mrs. Johnson tells me, "I found my cat last night."

* * *

"911?"

"This is not an emergency!"

"Okay, go ahead."

"I'm lost. I'm supposed to be at this thing at Shepherd of the Lake Church and I'm not from around here. I get so turned around when my husband's not with me."

"Where are you?"

"There's a big gray building that says 'Fortis.' I can't see any street signs. I feel so stupid."

"Are you on County Road B?"

"Yes! Yes."

"Do you know which way is east?"

"Yes."

"Take County Road B east past Fairview and you'll see it on your right-hand side."

"Oh, God bless you! God bless you. Thank you so much."

I hang up, feeling a lot more accomplished than I probably ought to. But I'm so excited. I got my first "thank you." And a "God bless you," to boot.

Joe Wilson

The last words Joe Wilson said to me, or anyone else, were: "This is bullshit." I didn't know what he meant when he said it. Bullshit that he had called 911? Bullshit that I kept asking him the same questions? Bullshit that he didn't understand me? That I didn't understand him?

I've only been out of training for a couple of months when Joe Wilson calls. On this evening, I'm sitting at console 36, which tends to be the spot where plebes get put because it's not vital that anyone sit there at all. I like console 36. Sitting there takes the pressure off. All I have to do is answer phones. I can't run registrations, I'm not needed on the main channel, and I'm only rarely on the fire channel. Console 36 is closest to the TV. You can watch "Jeopardy" and even put your feet on the counter if Chad isn't around.

It is somewhat busy for a Wednesday, so I'm picking up a lot of calls in rapid succession. At one point, my brother calls me on the non-emergency line wanting to know if I can baby-sit for him this Saturday. We get into a tiff about it, so I take a break to cool off, then come back to my console and started punching lines again.

"911?"

"Ramsey? This is Maplewood with a transfer. His name is Joe Wilson and he's at 725 Stockton Drive in Vadnais Heights. Go ahead, sir."

I sense uncertainty in the dispatcher's voice, like she knows she's sending me an odd call. Like she's glad this guy is out of her jurisdiction.

As soon as he starts talking, I know why. When I try to get Joe Wilson to confirm his address, he starts talking about his leg. He's calling on a cell phone, so I have nothing to go on but the address Maplewood gave me. When I ask him where he is, he slurs what sounds like "seventy-eight"-something Stockton, which I know doesn't exist. So I ask again. Instead of answering, he talks about how he is bleeding, how he has fallen from something. His words run together worse each second.

I picture a man lying on his back in his apartment somewhere in one of the many apartment buildings on Stockton. The buildings, I have learned, are close to the border of Vadnais Heights and Maplewood and would explain why his signal had bounced off a Maplewood tower and first went to Maplewood Dispatch. That is the extent of the technology our county offers. All I know is that Joe Wilson is somewhere within a couple miles of the address of the cell phone tower, whose location I now stare at longingly.

That, and I'm pretty sure he's drunk. He probably won't even remember this call tomorrow.

Just a few minutes after we are introduced, Joe Wilson grows tired of my questions. Right before he hangs up, he says, "This is bullshit."

With nothing better to go on, we send everyone to 725 Stockton Drive in Vadnais Heights. Two squads, several firefighters, and one ambulance each call out their arrivals to that house, and one by one, each report that nobody is home. I call the cell phone number back, but don't get an answer, or even a ring. Just a click.

One by one, they all clear out. No Joe Wilson to be helped.

I get out the phone book. By this time, I have begun answering other calls, but every little break I get, I look down to my lap and scan the white pages for a Joe Wilson on Stockton. I hope he'll be okay. I figure he will.

By mid-shift, I've given up on the phone book. By 11 PM, I've pretty much forgotten about Joe Wilson.

Two days later, on day shift, I catch the tail end of a conversation between Marlys and Kristen. There was a medical that Maplewood had passed on to us. They'd given us a bad address, Marlys tells Kristen, and we had sent police and medics, and he wasn't there.

But get this: It was some guy in Maplewood, not in Vadnais Heights. He was in the middle of moving day. His wife had gone ahead to the new house, while he had stayed behind at the old one. He had fallen off a ladder and fractured his leg. He bled to death.

Where was this? Kristen asks.

Marlys says, "Somewhere on Stockton Drive."

I stand up; I hear a ringing start in my ears.

"I took that call," I tell the room. "They transferred him. I talked to him. I took it." *He bled to death.*

I run out of dispatch, looking for Chad. When I find him, standing outside his office, there is a fire alarm sounding in my head. I tell him about Maplewood and Joe Wilson and how nobody helped him and he *bled to death.*

By this time, Marlys is standing next to me too. I want to put my hand on her shoulder in case I fall over, but I don't know her that well. Chad asks me, did you do this? Did you do that? Yes, I say. *Yes.*

Well, he says. "What else could you have done?"

"Oh, God."

I stand there and cry. I picture a different Joe Wilson than I had before, helpless and bleeding all his energy into the grass. Not drunk, as I had imagined, but delirious. Not passing out, but fading away.

I imagine his wife finding him there.

I cry over me. Pathetic, powerless, stupid me. Somewhere out in the cosmos was the question or the deduction or the method that would have located Joe Wilson. I can't help but think that if someone else had answered his call, that someone else would have known how to find him.

My skin hurts; my head hurts. I listen to the words that Chad and Marlys use to try to reassure me. I nod my head in agreement, but silently deflect all of it.

If I didn't do anything wrong, then why do I feel like this?

I tell Marlys I'm okay. I tell Chad I want to hear the tape once he finds it. Then I go back to work.

Back at my console, as raw as I am, I don't hate the work. I don't want to stop answering the phones. I don't want to go home. I am in a room with four other people who know—to one degree or another—exactly how this feels. I just want to sit and work next to them for the rest of the day.

For the next few hours, I fight and eventually lose to this overwhelming urge I have to look up Joe Wilson in the phone book again. Had I missed him? I scan the tiny lines in the white pages all over again. No Joe Wilson on Stockton. That gives me some comfort until I realize that I never thought to look up the spelling "Wilsen."

At the end of the shift, Chad tells me he listened to the tape. He has no problem with how I handled the call, he says. He also says it isn't a good idea that I listen to it. The best thing, he says, is to let it go. He says my mind is a dangerous place to be alone without supervision.

But at home, alone and away from the distraction of a ringing phone, I go there anyway. I can't help myself. Had I been kind? What had I said? How had I said it? I had thought he was drunk. Was I condescending? I was the last voice Joe Wilson ever heard. The weight of it overwhelms me.

I stay in that state of mind for the next couple of days, in the places that only exist in the past. The things you can't undo get lodged in the darkest corners of your mind, where nothing ever seems to get solved, just recycled into new anxiety.

I get pissed. I decide I was taken off training too soon.

I shouldn't be on my own yet. If Lily was still answering phones with me, she could shoulder half of this. I don't want it. I don't want to play this big a role in this big a play.

My husband gets home, it's Friday, and we do our best to move on with our weekend. Driving along a highway after having dinner out, I am startled when Jim suddenly pulls our van over.

"Do you see it?" He points to a full-grown doe that had been hit by a car. Its leg is fractured and the bone sticks out several inches. The animal scrapes itself toward the shoulder of an exit ramp, as if unaware of its own condition.

I turn away. I can't believe what I'm seeing.

Knowing the deer isn't going to live, Jim calls the local sheriff's office on his cell phone. A deputy arrives inside of five minutes with a shotgun. I watch from about twenty yards away as he takes aim, then shoots the deer four times. I listen carefully to the rounds as he squeezes them off. I want to know what a shotgun sounds like. Some day that might come in handy.

When Jim joins me back at the van, he grins at me like he had found something to be amused about in all of this. "What are you, the angel of death?" He kisses the back of my hand.

I am laughing and crying at the same time. I am crying over all the things I can't control, and maybe laughing because Joe is right.

This is bullshit.

Power Phones

I jump at the chance to take a course called simply "911 Dispatch" given by a company called Powerphone. After about the most *powerless* few months of my life, I'm not sure where the word *power* fits in with my line of work, except that it is ever present in the law enforcement image, in word, if not in deed. The image of the officer and the 911 operator is that of power and control. Call us and we'll step in and right the wrongs, fix the broken. We have the answers to the questions. We have the stuff and the things and we come in and we take control.

I'm hoping this three-day class will help me take control. Or at least give me some idea as to whom to transfer people, so somebody can somehow take control.

Our instructor is a tall, lean, career law enforcement machine in his fifties named George. He has the shaved-headed, muscular look of either a former Navy Seal or a track swimmer. He has a confident smile and a demeanor that says that nothing has *really* rattled him in a very long time. Outside of the shaven head, it's a look I envy. George looks like someone who is exactly where he's supposed to be.

There are moments that I love the job. When I get a medical or a domestic and my caller actually seems to benefit from whatever compassion I can give in the few minutes I have . . . that's when I love the job. When we get a theft call in progress and a witness helps us nab the guy, that's when I *freaking love* the job.

Then there's another part that still needs to be fed. It's the part that's still so scared of what waits for me at the other end of the line, on the other end of the microphone. I want to fill that space with the skill to handle anything, so it can stop growling and leave me be. Nobody's told me yet whether this kind of dispatch nirvana is impossible, so I keep hoping.

For the first time in a long time, I am getting urges to trip on acid. Though I gave up drinking when I gave up drugs, I also find myself yearning for the relaxing buzz of a good drink. After eleven years of sobriety, I am well aware of what triggers this. Stress and the unknown. I don't know whether I belong in this job. Along with that, I am still learning how to raise a now eleven-year-old girl who simply dropped into my lap one day like a big, beautiful, blue-eyed kitten.

Some days with her are so wonderful that I begin to

believe in destiny. Some days I feel the poor girl is the victim of a grand cosmic mistake for having to live with me. Those are the days when I can relate a little too deeply to some of my callers, who ask for officers to come over and make their children go to bed or get up and go to school. It's not that Lucy would ever behave that way, it's that sometimes, I am just that lost as to how to be a parent. When these people ask one of the officers I work with what to do, he likes to tell them, snidely, "You could try the parenting option." On a bad day, I fear I don't know what the parenting option is.

Those are the days when all my parenting skills, derived only from self-help books and phone conversations with my mother, simply slide out the window. Like when she comes home with head lice and all I want to do is run. What kind of mother does that? And I can't just let her subsist on popcorn and cold cereal and cookies, as I do. I have to make *suppers*. I resent that Jim doesn't make suppers. I resent that I can't spend all my money on a new pair of leather boots and leave $10 for groceries. I can't leave my book of erotic fiction on the coffee table. I can't make love when there's a child one wall away.

I am still too insecure to say out loud that I am either a mother or a dispatcher, yet I spend half my time worrying about how I am doing in each role. The fear with each is the same. "What if I make a mistake and someone gets hurt?"

On top of that, the two roles continually step on each other. As the low girl on the totem pole, I am relegated to afternoon shift: 3:00 to 11:00 PM, five days a week. I see Lucy most days for only twenty minutes before she goes off to school (and they're definitely *not* my best twenty minutes), and the rest of her life I get in updates from Jim.

As much as I want to be there for her, I often catch myself feeling happy about going off to work and not having to be there when she gets home from school. Though she's been with us almost two years, I still don't know what to say when she comes to me with certain problems. I'm not a person who likes to *play.* I don't watch cartoons. The last time I did a cartwheel, I hurt my lower back.

And *Jim.* It has only been a month on this new schedule, and Jim is already a little bit sore at me and a lot stressed out from being her only regular source of food, entertainment, and rides—and, of course, sounding board for all her preteen traumas.

I don't even ask what they eat for supper anymore. Don't want to know.

I worry about all the things that make us a strange, unconventional family, so drastically unlike the one I grew up in. I don't have a nine-to-five job, and I don't think I want one. I'm not the mother that my mother was. I don't revolve around Lucy, like my mother revolved around my brother and me. For all of this, I feel nothing but guilt.

When people ask me how things are going, I give them the Christmas card report. Her grades are great, she's got nice friends, and . . . hey, no cavities at the last checkup. Those things are all true. She *is* wonderful. She *is* normal. Therefore *I* must be the problem.

The therapist I began seeing when I started my new insurance with the county tells me that all of this is normal. What a rotten thing to say. He lets me cry it all out week after week in his windowless little office. He gives me brochures for groups that could help, parenting classes. It's all I can do just to get my butt to work every day, but I always tell him I'll try to sign up for one or two. In reality, there's a big part of me that doesn't want to put in any more work to be a good mom. Maybe parenting is something you're either good at or you're just *not.*

But 911 class is different. There's hope for me here. There's a formula for how to be the perfect dispatcher. There has to be.

I arrive early for each class and sit next to Danielle and Casey, two dispatchers I work with. Danielle is a mother of two boys, one in first grade, one in kindergarten. She tells me about her project for the week: She's decorating the boys' rooms with a Batman theme. Casey is a single guy, constantly overflowing with tales of conquest (or not) and tales of drunkenness (or hangover).

I sit in between them. I envy how completely Danielle seems to have her shit together, balancing work and motherhood like a pro. I envy Casey for how out of control his life is. No balance. And no one to have to explain it to. But what I really want, more than anything is what George has: knowledge, skill, control, *power!*

We learn about ways to handle all manner of crises. We listen to recordings that I imagine have taken several years to collect. There are many examples of what not to do in certain situations, and no examples of perfect dispatching.

We listen to a male dispatcher talk to a young woman who is suicidal. Before he plays the tape, George tells us to listen for things we would change. This is not difficult.

During the conversation, he puts her on hold several times. Once, when he returns to her, he asks, "Do you feel better yet?" as though there is a limit to how long a woman can feel suicidal. He doesn't relate to her or listen to her. I don't like him very much until I realize that he is the lone dispatcher for his area, answering officers on the main channel, as well as other 911 calls . . . all while trying to keep this woman on the phone and get her location. And oh, by the way, please don't kill yourself, ma'am.

Regarding this call, George tells us that it costs nothing to empathize with our callers. I write that in my notebook, which is otherwise blank. It is a simple concept, but to me, very powerful. You don't have to have ten years under your belt or work the day shift or dispatch on the main channel to have compassion, to show empathy. Near as I can tell, it's the best tool I've got.

We listen to a call in which a man calls 911 to let them know that he's going to shoot himself. The man's voice is angry, challenging. He doesn't want to be talked out of it, he just called because he doesn't want his wife to be the one to find him. He tells the operator his location, that he's parked there in a maroon Buick, and again, that he's going to blow his own head off. We listen to a shotgun blast.

After this call, George offers very little. There is no solution to this call. It's just part of the job. And now, part of us.

We listen to a call that is like a riddle. A woman calls for police because her new husband and her teenage son are fighting. There is also a four-year-old girl in the house. In a fit of rage, the husband takes out a gun and shoots his stepson, his wife, and then himself.

We learn from George that the little girl is now trapped in a room inside the house, blocked from leaving by the father's dead body. We hear the child begin to cry, then pick up the phone that was dropped by the mother and begin dialing a number. We listen to the beeps of a push-button phone. When the operator finally gets her attention, the child is starting to whimper.

We learn that the operator has no location information for this house, and that now she is going to have to find a way to extract that information from a small child who is likely in shock. What follows are several attempts to get clues from the girl, which eventually pay off. The child tells her they live on an island; there is only one in the area. This narrows it down. The child tells her about a red car in the driveway. Also good to know. Officers begin circling the island with their sirens on, until, at last, the sounds can be heard by the operator on the phone.

It takes about thirty minutes to find the house.

George gives us a chance to think about what solution was missed that might have located the child right away. I try, but I can't think. My brain is filled the sound of a screaming child.

Other students offer up some guesses, but George has stumped us.

"What number was the child dialing?" George rests his hands on his waistline. "The operator never asked what number she was trying to call." If she had, George tells us, she would have found the child's grandparents, who could have told them the address.

It's a brilliant little piece of problem solving, but when he tells us this, all I can think about is having to inform someone's parents that their daughter, grandson, and son-in-law are all dead. And by the way, can you head over there and pick up the four-year-old while we pull the bodies out?

I'm not finding the solutions I had hoped for. Instead, I see that there is no one way to do the job we do. No easy way.

George is a never-ending font of mind-bending, heart-wrenching calls: officers down, children trapped in burning buildings, gunshots, gunshots, gunshots. After day two, my mind and heart are numb from all the trauma, suffering, and death. He reminds us that most of what we're hearing are calls that only happen once or twice in a career. But we're not working the switchboard at IBM, here. Sooner or later, we'll get one. How will we handle it?

It's rare, George tells us, that dispatchers are given the same opportunities as officers and paramedics to "debrief" after a traumatic incident. By that, he means that some departments give their officers a chance to talk about what happened together in an informal setting, facilitated by a counselor or chaplain. It's a chance to grieve. More than that, it's acknowledgment that there is something to be grieved. Most departments don't see the need for their dispatchers to have the same kind of outlet, even though dispatchers, too, may feel a certain amount of post-traumatic stress.

I think about Joe Wilson when he says it. I still think about him almost every day. Would I still think about him if I had been properly debriefed? I wonder. I'm not being sarcastic. I really want to know. What if I were able to forget? Would that make me feel better?

I imagine sitting in one of these classes five years in the future and unexpectedly hearing Joe Wilson's voice and mine, in one of George's series of recordings. I wonder how it would look to others. I wonder what there is to be learned.

I'm drained. After three full days, I learn that there are many more ways to do this thing wrong than right. I learn that compassion costs nothing. Yet, if I have the chance, I'll take more classes like these. Since there is no formula to follow, I figure I'm going to have to keep soaking up everything I can. Each call I take or listen to is like turning over the pieces of a puzzle. I may have to look at them many times before I start to see where they belong.

The best thing, though, is that all three classes take place during the day. For three afternoons in a row, I am home when Lucy gets home from school, just like a real mom. Twice, I make supper. Neither supper is popcorn. On the second night, she devours the spaghetti from the jar and the instant garlic bread and says, "Wow. You're a really good cook!"

On the afternoon of day three, I take a brief test, which I pass, and I earn my Powerphone Certificate. I am now officially ready to go back and do whatever it was I was doing before, but perhaps just a little bit better.

Lily

As a dispatcher, I want to *be* Lily. In one night, with only four dispatchers on duty (there are normally five on a summer afternoon), we suddenly had a police chase and a hostage situation take place at the same time. We sent out an alpha-page for any dispatchers nearby to come in and help. Lily arrived after only about ten minutes, and with all of nearly twenty of our phone lines ringing and one possibly armed suspect still unaccounted for, I was so happy to see her, I almost cried. I wanted to bend down and kiss her feet.

She knew what to do, whom to call, and she could handle whatever was about to happen on the main channel. Those kinds of skills take years.

Lily manages to be wildly valuable in her job with

only a minimum of pissiness. She's kind to her callers, but she's nobody's stooge. You don't repeat yourself to Lily; she heard you the first time. "Yeah," she'll say, "I got that part."

As a trainer, she's a total ball breaker, but if you do your job well, she'll tell you. If you don't, she'll tell you, "Pull your head out of your ass." When she doesn't like what you have to say, she'll growl, "Stop saying things!"

And my favorite Lily-ism is "Garbage in, garbage out." This translates to: You took that piece-of-shit call, now you can dispatch it yourself.

Lily taught me that sometimes you have to get out of the room, find your brain, stuff your heart back into your pocket where it was before it spilled out, then go back in and do your job. Don't be a hero. Don't be a social worker. Take a lot of vitamins; get lots of sleep. Want some carrots? Have a carrot. You'll feel better.

It seems that dispatching somehow shaped her personality, yet I can't imagine how she ever could have been different. She was meant to do this, yet I can see her easily living without it.

Lily doesn't look like a dispatcher, if such a *look* can be identified. Her appearance defies the unhealthy living trap that most dispatchers seem to fall into. She is tall and slender, with healthy tanned skin, all despite nearly ten years of sitting for long hours in the dankness and hungry boredom of a 911 call center. She wears plastic flowers in her hair. She wears rings on fingers that other people don't often wear rings on, and she can wear dark brown and still be the most noticeable woman in the room.

If I didn't like her so much, I would hate her guts.

* * *

Once Lily had to scream at a woman whose son was hanging from a tree. She said twice that she doesn't feel bad about it, yet it strikes me that she is not just telling me this, but reminding herself. Reminding herself not to feel bad about it.

Like me, Lily tries to write about what it's like. After a really wild night, she goes home and writes it, and vomits it out and tries to tell about *it*. She tries to capture the feeling of what you find yourself doing. That sometimes you have to scream at people in their worst times—slap them over the phone—to get them to do what needs to be done. Then it's how you feel about it afterward. Slapped.

Theresa first answered the call, and the mother was hysterical. Her fourteen-year-old son was hanging from a tree. Theresa was trying to calm her the best way she could think of.

"Ma'am, police are on the way. You need to calm down . . . I know, I know . . ."

When Lily tried to cut in, Theresa said, "No, I have it." Theresa had bonded to it. She took it. She started it. She wanted it. Dropping it, in that moment, would betray the call in some way. Or the caller.

Which is it, the caller or the call? Lily asks. Which are we bonded to? Either way, Lily had to break it.

Over Theresa, Lily yelled at the mother, "Ma'am, get a grip. YOU NEED TO GET A GRIP TO HELP HIM! Go get a knife or a garden shears and cut him down right now."

She yelled at a woman whose son had hung himself.

But because of Lily, the mother whose son had hung

himself dropped the phone and tried to save him. Lily then spoke to the boy's eleven-year-old brother, who was busy trying to keep his six-year-old sister from peeking out the window at the scene under the tree.

But Mom didn't save him. Lily didn't save him. Theresa didn't save him. He was gone long before all of that. And before all that yelling. All that talking, all that bonding . . . all that cutting.

Theresa might have been sore at Lily for cutting into her call, but I doubt it. There are plenty of things dispatchers bicker about with each other. *You're not picking up enough calls. You drank all the coffee. You forgot to call for the tow truck.* But there's no bickering about the boy-hanging-from-a-tree call. There's no way to make it better or worse. It's been shared. It's just two women, two mothers, who, without ever seeing it, were witness to the death of a child.

At least, Lily says, the mother can know that she tried to do something. "Am I trying to make myself feel better? Maybe. But I don't think so."

Lily's also the one who reminded me about free will, after my first suicide. You can't change it. It's just out there and you can't control it. For some people, she says, there just aren't enough trees.

* * *

It's not that Lily doesn't eat junk food. She can put away half a quart of cookie dough ice cream with the best of them. I'd like to think *I* taught her that, but I don't know.

For a while there, Lily and I got into the habit of sending someone for ice cream almost every night. Carrots are fine, but ice cream is a great stress reliever during those long summer nights when everybody's garages are catching on fire and everybody whose garage is not currently in flames wants to pick a fight with their respective spouses. Ice cream works well for dispatchers because you can answer the phone or the radio with a mouthful of softserve and nobody can tell. No chewing.

It was a sad night in the comm center when I logged onto the Dairy Queen web site and leaned how many hundreds of calories are in one small malted shake. Some people don't eat that many calories all day long.

I tried to tell Lily, but she put her hands over her ears like a child and yelled, "Stop saying things!"

Oh well. Garbage in, garbage out.

Good Neighbors

I know a lot about my neighbors that sometimes, I would rather not.

I know things like the guy in 2210 on our street doesn't get along with the guy at 2205, so they call the cops on each other constantly over code violations and noise complaints. 2210 sometimes leaves his dog outside barking too long, probably just to piss off 2205.

I know that the lady in 2450, around the corner and one block down, tried to kill her husband with a knife when she found out he had a mistress. She didn't go to jail. The day after it happened, she was outside raking leaves with a passion you don't often see in a homeowner performing simple yard work.

I know that the teenage daughter in a house two

blocks from ours dates a man from two hours north of the city who once told his young girlfriend that he had a gun and was going to kill himself if she tried to break up with him. She didn't, so he didn't.

I know that only a few houses away from us in a cute pinkish split-level lives a twenty-something man and his elderly grandmother. "Jacob" has some sort of emotional disorder that causes him to fly into violent rages. He has sent his grandmother to the hospital more than once. She doesn't press charges because she feels sorry for him. I wave to her when I see her out in the yard, weeding. Someday, I think, he'll kill her.

My daughter walks past that house every day before and after school. One day I tell her, if the man at that house ever tries to talk to you, let me know. He's troubled, I tell her. He's gotten in trouble with the police. I am vague, of course, because I don't want to give her all the gory details.

I don't know what I'm trying to accomplish in telling her this. I just don't want to find her eating milk and cookies over there some day. I just don't think he needs to be her *friend.*

One night, Lucy comes home after playing with a girl who lives across the street. She's breathing heavily and is all excited. "We were walking down the street," she pants, "and we saw a car coming, and then he saw us, and then he swerved way around us and it was so freaky! I know it was that one guy up the street," she says. "We ran as fast as we could!"

"What kind of a car?"

"Um, I don't know."

He drives an SUV. And even if it *was* him, he was

probably just trying not to hit the two little girls in the road. I've turned him into the boogey-man. This, I regret. He's probably not a dangerous guy in general, as long as you're not his grandmother.

It's hard to know where to use these things I know and when to leave them be. But what would you do if you knew your child was home alone, and only eight houses away from her, about twenty police officers and drug enforcement agents were setting up a perimeter in order to catch a man with a felony narcotics warrant? Would you call her and tell her to lock the doors?

I didn't. After an hour-long standoff, the suspect was cornered in his house and taken to jail. Lucy and the rest of the neighborhood were none the wiser.

Lucky them.

* * *

Every once in a while, I get a call from the street that my parents live on. When I see "Mill Lane" on my computer screen, it stops my heart for a second. The first time it happened, I realized that some day, one of my parents may need an ambulance to come and help in some way. If they do, I may be the one to have to send it.

* * *

My husband and I own rental property: one single-family house on Linda Avenue. Right from the start, we found that being landlords was much more hard work and expense than we had predicted. We hang onto it in the hopes that in several years, our hard work will begin to pay off. But good renters are rare.

You would think, given where I work, that I would be

able to tell the gems from the jackasses. Whenever I find myself in need of a new renter, I always mention it to all my cop and dispatcher friends in the hopes that somebody will know somebody halfway decent who wants to rent the house. But because most of my co-workers prefer to live outside the county they work in, for reasons that are becoming more and more clear to me, they usually just nod their heads and wish me luck. Then they say something I wish I had listened to much more carefully *before* we became landlords: "Isn't being a landlord an awful lot of work?"

Not at all! I tell them. Want to buy some rental property?

"So, do you have a new renter yet?" Andrea asks me one night.

I tell her that yeah, I got this new guy who's going to live there with his three kids. He's newly divorced. Seems like a good egg.

"Good for you," she says. "Cool."

A call comes in, from a cell phone.

"911?"

"I want the police to come over here. I want this guy off *my property*."

"What's your address?"

"393 Linda Avenue."

(Beat.)

"I'm sorry . . . uh . . . could you repeat that address, please?"

"393 Linda Avenue!"

"Okay. Okay. What's your name?"

"Jonathon."

Jonathon, the man who had signed a six-month lease

with me less than a month before, had a new girlfriend who had an old jealous husband and a new baby (the husband's), and this was a big ol' messed up love triangle being played out on my front lawn, in full view of everybody.

When I run the license plate of the van that the unwanted old husband had driven to *my house*, it comes back to a guy with a felony warrant for violating the conditions of his predatory sex offender probation. *Predatory sex offender.*

I send not just one or two, but three squads over to my house. I'm sure the neighbors are thrilled. Almost as thrilled as they were when they found out they were going to be living next to rental property.

When police arrive, they find no predatory sex offender. It was just his brother, who had borrowed his car. Bet he won't do that again.

"Dispatch to 465, your status?"

"Code 4. Party's leaving and has been advised."

"Advised" used in this context is cop talk for *better not see your face here again during my shift, asshole.*

"Copied. 22:10."

I sit back from the radio console and stretch my arms over my head. The dull chronic shoulder pain I have developed on the job has suddenly turned into ten daggers, all stabbing the muscle simultaneously.

"So, that was my rental house, then."

Andrea's big brown eyes get wide.

"Oh."

"Yeah."

"Well, at least the felony warrant guy wasn't there."

"Yeah! That's good, anyway."

"Uh-huh."

"Did he know it was you?"

"Don't know."

If he did, he certainly never brought it up when he was dropping off his rent check.

* * *

"911?"

"Yes, I'd like to report a suspicious person in my neighborhood. I live in the Wentworth Development."

Some residents in the newer areas of the county identify themselves to us as being from a certain *development.* I wonder what is next. Will we all begin carrying ID badges stating how much we paid for our homes, what kind of cars we drive, and whether our pets are purebred?

"What's this person doing?"

"He's walking down Deer Path Road toward the park."

"What's he doing that's suspicious?"

"Well, I've never seen him before."

"But is he doing anything we should be worried about?"

"Well, he's walking really slowly . . ."

"Anything else?"

"I just don't think he's from around here. I've lived here a long time."

"About how old is he?"

"Mmm, twenties . . ."

"What's he wearing?"

"Baggy jeans and a baseball cap."

I think I already know the answer to this, but what the hell: "Is he a white male?"

"Black."

"Okay, ma'am, we'll check the area."

I pop the call into the pending cue and wait for the inevitable protest from Marsha, who will now have to broadcast this little turd. The type code that I attach to it is "SUS" for suspicious. I can't help but think there should be a more appropriate code we could institute, like maybe "WWB." Walking While Black.

Once Casey, who is black, took a similar call in which the caller described the "suspect" as being "colored."

"What color is he?" Casey asked.

Friends in High Places

One night I return to my house after running errands, open my front door, and find a terrible burning smell. The air inside is thick and hazy.

I am alone, except for my three cats and my dog. I quickly herd two angry cats and one confused chocolate lab onto our screen porch. There is one cat left to find, but instead I start looking for the source of the smoke and the smell.

I run from room to room: first the master bedroom, then the office, then Lucy's room, then back to the living room. Meanwhile the smelly haze is starting to bug me and I'm getting lightheaded. I do the whole tour over again, from room to room. Where's it coming from? My eyes are starting to hurt.

I start opening doors and windows. I look around for the fire extinguisher. But I don't even know where the fire is. Then I think about looking in all the rooms one more time. I wonder where cat number three could be. I wonder if my house is going to burn to the ground. My head is starting to spin. My eyes sting.

Crap. I'm trying not to call 911. I have to call 911.

"911?"

Now, Kendra, a coworker of mine, is likely staring at a screen with either my name or my husband's name, our address, and our phone number.

"Um, hi. Uh, this is Caroline."

"Caroline? Honey, what's wrong?"

I tell her about the haze and the smell, and pretty soon she sounds as worried as I feel. I've not heard her like this before. Then again, I've never called her like this before.

She tells me that the fire department is coming, then she says, "So, you know the rules."

"Uh, yeah." I say. I'm sure I do, but for a few seconds I'm too freaked out to remember what the hell she's referring to. Oh, yeah! We always tell people to get out of the house. *That* rule. But like a typical caller, I don't follow her instructions right away. Instead I check one last thing: the dishwasher.

When I open it, a concentrated wave of the stench of burning plastic hits me right in the face. Eureka! Instant headache. Now, I'm going outside. It's too late to cancel the fire brigade, and I know it. So I take my cordless phone with me and wait. My husband, who's at work, calls me at that moment.

"Oh, hi, honey. I can't talk. I've got the fire department coming over."

"Why? Some kind of get-together or something?"

"No, the house is on fire or something."

"What?"

"Don't worry, I think it's the dishwasher. Oop. Gotta go. I see someone coming up the hill right now."

"Red lights and sirens?"

"Of course."

"Oh, honey."

In only a minute, Fire Officer Mike pulls three separate but equally charred pieces of what used to be a rubber spatula out of the bottom of my dishwasher. I wanna die.

"Don't be so embarrassed!" he says. "That's what we're here for."

He gets on his portable radio and tries to cancel the rest of the fire crew, but it's too late. I look outside to see Fire Engine Number 9, about as big as an eighteen-wheeler and red as you please, lumbering down my normally quiet street. And behind Fire Engine Number 9 is Deputy Marnie Dunley, pulling up in her squad. My humiliation is complete.

"2460 you can cancel!" I say, as I walk up to her squad.

"Ten-four. What the hell are ya doing?"

Marnie is grinning happily at me because cops love it when people do stuff they can give them shit about later. We jaw for a few minutes, then she rolls away to whatever awaits her next.

I take my cordless phone and go back inside. Another satisfied customer.

Anniversary

Everyone promised this first year would suck. Sometimes when I hear that, I wonder, then why am I doing it? Some days the best I can come up with is that I have to do *something*.

After about a year on the job, I know just enough about the job to be dangerous. I've heard a lot of calls. I've noticed certain patterns. I've heard some really awful things. I think I'm pretty smart.

At the root of it is the desire to make sense of the vast minefield of things I still don't understand. Things I never even knew took place. Why do mothers call their children motherfuckers? Why do people adopt dogs, then starve and beat them? Why do children destroy expensive Porta Potties for no good reason? Why do grown men want to have sex with little children? Why do couples have children, then fail to care for them?

I'm almost as confused by those questions as I am with some of the people I work with. Cops and dispatchers wear many different faces. Some will show you a dozen of them at different times in one eight-hour shift. Some of their faces are cruel and unfeeling. Some are highly intellectual. Some are deeply caring.

I am developing my faces, too. There is one face that I brought with me from my other life, my life pre-911. It's the sarcastic brat who likes to rant. It's great for law enforcement, I'm finding. It finds humor in even sick situations. It can snipe back at other people's ugly faces without letting on how hurt I am.

My sensitive face, also one that I brought with me, is the one that's going to have to go. It's the one that gets all hurt when Lily smacks my hand away from pushing the wrong button. It's the one that expects kindness, and can't let go of the expectation.

* * *

Steve:

Just so there's no misunderstanding, when you and I talk about work-related stuff in the comm center, I don't intend to put up with sarcastic remarks, or you making comments under your breath at me.

If you have a problem with a call I have entered or if you disagree with something I've done, then let me know without making an ass out of me in front of everyone. That's all I want. And if that's just something you do with everyone, then I suggest you stop. It's not winning you any friends.

Caroline

I print my little note, then my computer asks me if I want to save it. Sure. I call it takenoshit.wpd. Staring at my computer, I look back over the words. The writing of them has calmed me down a bit, but not much. I know they're not going to change anything, or anybody. I've taken plenty of shit since I started this job. Some of it I deserved, but a lot of it I didn't.

I've complained to Chad once or twice, which helped for a little while. It's not personal, he assures me every time. This happens to everybody. Please don't quit. It'll get better.

There is a tendency in this line of work, especially with those who have a lot of tenure, to become impatient, intolerant, and often cruel to dispatchers with less experience under their belts. On this particular night, I am more sick of it than usual. Every time I tried to talk to him, Steve responded with a condescending edge in his voice. He is making sure everyone in the room knows what a drag it is for him to have to put up with my inexperience.

Steve really doesn't have that much tenure, but he just came off of two nights in a row with Kristen, who treated him pretty much the way he treated me. Sarcasm. It's the gift that keeps on giving.

Kristen dispatched for police long before 911 even existed. She has been there so long that nobody who worked for the sheriff's department can remember a time when she *wasn't* the way she is. In fact, most could recall when she was worse.

The funny thing is, some days she and I can gab for half an hour at a time about the things we have in common. We both love old houses. We even talked once about what it would be like to buy an old house and renovate it together.

Then one day later, I'm back to crying into my headset over some belittling thing she said.

People tell me this job will help me learn to stand up for myself. I don't know what to make of that, honestly. Is there a class I can take? I'll gladly take it. But I'm not the one who treats people like shit. Is there a class for people who treat people like shit? I'll take my class if they take theirs.

How do you get away with treating people like shit on this job? We're all union members employed by a government agency, which means it practically takes an act of Congress for any of us to be fired after having been on the job longer than a year. At least, that's what I'm told.

But, beyond that, there's a certain mentality in law enforcement that says you shouldn't be the type of person who takes things personally. If you are, you're weak. Build a wall. I hear that one a lot. The problem is, I'm a person. And when another person calls me on the phone asking for my compassion and my help, I don't want them to have to jump my wall to get it.

One night, I snapped at Kristen for something strange. I was in a mood. But once it came out, I couldn't believe it. I had snapped at Kristen. I sent her an e-mail, apologizing. I didn't know how to stand up for myself yet, but I figured I could at least keep my own slate clean. It's how I keep my sanity. God forbid thirty years from now, I should ever think it normal to treat a newcomer the way I've been treated at this job.

Thirty years on the job? Twenty-nine more years like the year I just had? Oy.

I never gave Steve that note.

Jurisdiction

Jurisdiction is a huge deal. One of the first things an operator always asks a caller is, "Where did it happen?" or "Where are you?" Number one, we have to know that above any other thing before we can help you, and number two, we have to know if we're the ones who are supposed to render said help. The lesser-known third reason is that if your problem, dilemma, or whatever, is out of our jurisdiction, we can safely usher you to the right agency and . . . ahem . . . not have to do anything more.

Jurisdiction is a nitpicky thing, and it's often a source of conflict between police and sheriff's departments. Counties and cities that border one another all like to gripe about how so-and-so tried to send us a call that wasn't ours, or so-and-so tried to take a call that wasn't theirs. Determining jurisdiction can also lead to some pretty tense conversations between callers and call-takers.

"911?"

"Yeah, there's just been a three-car accident on Mead Road and Hodges."

"Is it on Mead Road or Hodges?"

"Mead Road."

"What direction were they heading on Mead Road?"

"One was going west and the other two were going east, I guess. What does that matter?"

"It's a border street."

"Well just send someone, for God's sake!"

Inside the comm center, we have our own borders as well. Though not as clearly defined. When Marlys works, she is on the data channel. There is no special contract with the county on that. There's no sign. It's just a house rule.

And Kristen rules the main channel.

After thirty-three years on the job, there is no question as to where Kristen sits when she arrives for a shift in the comm center. She is the main. To the officers at the other end of the radio, she is as calm and collected dispatching a suicide in progress as she is if it were a theft report. She makes sure every possible question is answered before she sends officers; she won't accept "I don't know" for an answer. Nor will she accept "I'm sorry" as an excuse.

In the chair next to her sits one person who serves as backup to the main. This person is almost *never* me. On the nights that Kristen is off duty, I am gradually learning the main by backing up Marsha or Lily. I'm told I do okay. I'm told the main is just something you learn by *doing*.

One night, much too early in this process, I sit myself down next to Kristen at the beginning of the shift. Lily, who is about to leave for the day, spots me. "Watcha doing?"

I pull out of my slouch to face her; I'm confident. "I think I can handle it. I do."

"Yeah . . . not just yet," Lily says. "Trust me."

Thank God. I was only sitting there so people wouldn't think I was afraid. But now, I've been given permission to stay away. Nay, I've been *ordered* to stay away. After this, I go out of my way to avoid sitting next to Kristen, ever. Sometimes, this means coming to work thirty minutes early to claim any other of the three seats available. I am chicken. Sue me.

But then one afternoon, it happens. There is only one place to sit. Steve and Lisa are both firmly planted at their stations, Steve with his personal laptop and his super-sized quarter-pounder meal, and Lisa with her knitting. Lily is not around to save me.

I sit cautiously, as if I might break the chair. Kristen glances my way, then looks around the room and at the other two dispatchers, says nothing.

Wherever you go, there you are.

Fine. I'll do it. I want to be broken in. I'm tired of being afraid of Kristen. I'm tired of pretending that I don't belong on "her main" (as she calls it). I'm going to do just fine, I tell myself.

But it is not to be. I am tight as a drum, and I start messing up right away. I step on her transmissions. I answer the phone too much, she tells me. She wants me available to back her up, not sitting on 911 all the time. So I stay off the phones and try to back her up. But she doesn't need the help, so I sit like a moron, afraid to dispatch on the main, afraid to answer the phone, certain that my other two colleagues are wondering why I'm *not doing anything*. I'm afraid to breathe. My shoulders are on fire.

Around 1800, someone calls in a domestic in the parking lot of one of the local grocery stores. But it is a grocery store that sits on a city border, and as Kristen dispatches it, we get word that the couple has gotten into their vehicle and are headed out of our jurisdiction into Maplewood. Someone should call Maplewood police. Kristen is on the main, Steve is on the phone with the witness, and Lisa is on a different call altogether.

I should be calling Maplewood, but I don't realize that right away. I am waiting for Kristen to tell me what to do. I am afraid to do anything else. She glares at me, punches an outgoing line, and calls them herself.

Shit.

Three minutes later, when it's over, she turns her chair toward me and says, "I can't do everything. You're supposed to *back me up*. If you can't handle the job, you should let someone else sit there."

I am out of my jurisdiction. I don't know what to say. I know she's right. And I know she's wrong. All I want to do is cry. She shudders at the wide-eyed, pathetic look on my face. I am too weak to rebut her, and she hates that. "Get yourself together," she tells me. "I'm going outside to smoke."

My Marsha

Marsha is a big blond woman with movie-star eyes and a man's throaty laugh, and she laughs a lot. She is one of my favorite things to see when I get to work. Mostly because of how kind she's been to me, and partly because if she's sitting on the main, it means Kristen is off duty.

Marsha is becoming a friend of mine. She's not someone I would typically get close to; she says things like "no bigger than a minute" and attaches her belief that "God always has a plan" to every life crisis you can think of, from weight gain to terminal cancer. I'm ten times more cynical than she is, yet she's been at this job more than ten times longer.

When I get pissy on the job, she turns to me, breathes

a deep breath in, and says, "In with the butterflies, out with the dragons!" which drives me crazy, because I take myself *way* too seriously to let a silly mantra like that ruin the foul mood I've let someone put me in.

Marsha doesn't want to be a dispatcher forever, but she doesn't know what else she can do that pays this well and offers this kind of security. She has a four-year-old boy and a mortgage and windows that need replacing.

In her free time, Marsha writes children's books and short fiction. Somewhere between the rinse cycle and the dryer is when she gets time for that. Or just between dropping off her son for a play date and picking him up two hours early because he's having a tantrum. She's a tortured writer who dreams about a ten-thousand-copy first run and a book signing at Barnes & Noble, just like me.

One night, she invites me to her house, where we're going to pluck my eyebrows, drink coffee, and dish. Marsha is an expert plucker, with perfectly sculpted ash-blonde brows. She wacks away at my unibrow with quick little tugs, while simultaneously explaining to her son why he shouldn't dance the lambada on their kitchen table just right now.

"Mitchell!" Marsha says, raising her inside voice. "I'm thinking it's time for your nap."

This causes a scream, which leads to a tantrum, which ends with a nap. Marsha returns after putting Mitchell in his room, and begins plucking anew. My eyes are sore and beginning to water, but I let her keep going.

Now that we're alone, there's something I must know. It's something that sticks in my cluttered, overwhelmed head every day. Whether I'm at work or not.

When will I get it?

"Get what?" She is plucking at the hairs that are above the middle of my left eye, and it hurts like a bastard.

"When did you get to the point where you didn't feel like an idiot?"

She laughs from deep down inside. "You do. You will."

"I will what?"

Mercifully, she rests her plucking hand on the table. Then she looks me in the eye for a long, meaningful moment. This is another thing she does that drives me crazy. "You worry too much, Beautiful."

"Okay . . . Gorgeous."

Marsha is one of the few people I've met in this job who has actually had formal postsecondary training as a 911 dispatcher. When she tells me that, I wonder, how can you prepare a room full of students how to act when Mom shoots herself in the head in front of her three children? How do you train for that?

After her formal training, Marsha interned at the county, then a few months later got a call asking if she would like a job there. One of their dispatchers had shot himself in the head. She accepted; they gave her his old locker.

I wonder why she isn't cynical like me, and like so many others I work with who have been their forever and have every right to be cynical, unlike me.

"I've come full circle with all of that," she says. "Every call is different. Who am I to judge the people who call me?"

Some of us, I guess, move in a circle at this job, and end up back where we started. Happy to serve, content to do our best and not judge. Some of us move in a straight line. The end is just an end. It ends because we have burned out. I wonder which one I'll be.

Marsha is one of the few people I know who sounds completely natural calling perfect strangers "honey" and "dear" on the phone. That's not really my style, but it I admire how intimate she can be with perfect strangers, and how they, in general, eat it with a spoon. She has retained the one thing that the job seems to have stripped from everyone else I've seen: patience.

Another of my coworkers is so routinely impatient with callers that she doesn't even bother to find out what they're calling about most of the time. She seems to already know. Except when she doesn't. When she doesn't like what she's hearing, she interjects with a whiplash "*Ma'am*" or "*Sir*" in the condescending tone of a nun dressing down a third-grade boy who has forgotten his homework. Then two minutes later, her boyfriend calls, and she is all sweetness and light.

Every once in a while, I hear rumblings about Marsha being too nice to the dispatchers working under her. She doesn't take charge enough, she lets people slack off, smart off, whatever. All I have to say about any of that is that I don't friggin' care. What would you rather have people say about you at the end of your life? "She was too kind"? Or "She was a stone-cold bitch"?

Kristen

Kristen and I can talk about old houses: what we could do to improve them, renovate, decorate. She and her brother have inherited a house from their mother. It is a run-down turn-of-the-century two-and-a-half story in a St. Paul neighborhood now dotted with rental houses and gang crash pads.

Knowing they have to sell the house, the two siblings have renovated it room by room. For months and months, they put all their after-work energy into the project. It had been an arduous process, during which, Kristen tells me, she realized her brother is every bit the perfectionist ball buster that she is, and possibly even more.

It takes me by surprise to hear her say it. I didn't know she knew.

When the house is ready to sell (but not perfect, by Kristen's estimation), she encourages me to check it out. Her real estate agent holds an open house. Because the renovation has been so radical, the agent has old pictures of the house on hand for anyone who is curious. The old hardwood floors had huge dark spots and gouges, and the old built-in cabinetry had been painted over. It had been a garbage house.

Kristen and her brother, by stripping, sanding, finishing, and rebuilding, have completely renewed each floor and cabinet. Every detail has been attended to, including the light switches and sockets. Every inch of wood has been polished to shine, and every fixture is new, yet still beautifully brassy and old. Kristen even took a class in how to make stained glass just so she could add her colorful designs to the front entry and on the glasswork in the dining room.

She had approached the house as she approached her work. She had been painstaking and perfectionist and relentless. Anything less would not have been acceptable.

It is perfect. I even think about whether I can afford to buy the place, then remember about the neighborhood.

Kristen has made something beautiful in a place where there had been none. I can look at her differently, knowing that. Still, she scares me to death.

* * *

I complain about my hours constantly. Once a month, when Chad posts the schedule, I see on paper all the missed outings and long nights, and I throw another pity party about it. Gina, also a mom, joins me.

I'm missing all of Lucy's softball games because of work.

Jim and I haven't been on a "date" in months.

Gina echoes my complaints. She has three boys she almost never sees.

From the opposite side of the room, Kristen pipes in. She has worked afternoons, more or less, for more than thirty years.

"I practically raised my children by phone," she says.

That shuts my mouth.

I don't know if I could make that kind of sacrifice. I wonder if it was a conscious decision on her part, or just a slow, steady slipping away of the years. I wonder if she, like me, fantasized about bigger better things. I wonder, but I don't ask.

Maybe she just knew that what she was doing needed to be done. And that she was meant to be the one to do it, regardless of what it did to her personally, to her family, to her ability to have a "normal life."

For the first time since I've known Kristen, I want to thank her for being a 911 operator. I want to thank her the same way that you would thank a soldier for giving his or her life for freedom. But I don't. It's almost more difficult to imagine than standing up to her.

Coppers

Dear Lord, please protect Brian from whoever he's fighting with right now, please, Lord, please let this end well, please give him the strength to overpower them, please God help him . . . God please give him strength, God please. . . .

When the struggle started, I alerted Kristen, who quickly announced on the main channel that 2230 needed help at the Maple Inn, Room 100. Now there are something like five more squads burning across town to help him. But I'm beginning to learn about all the things that can happen in minutes. Minutes and seconds.

I am listening to those seconds on the other end of 2230's cell phone. He had called me to check if these two guys had any warrants. He was going to arrest them for cocaine possession, and they were cooperating, at first. He had them sitting on the beds in the hotel room.

Now I am clutching the earpiece on my headset as if my ability to hear what's happening to 2230, known to his friends and family as *Brian,* can somehow change the course of things. I am praying like my mother used to pray at her prayer desk over the seriously ill. It's all I know to do because I'm out of practice. *Dear Lord,* she would say, *Dear Lord, please wrap your arms around so-and-so and give him the strength to overcome such-and-such. . . .*

For an eternity, Brian and the two men fight. It's the grunting of physical force and the sounds of body parts hitting body parts, and stomping on the floor, and then it's silence. I'm helpless. I'm helpless. I can't help him. Except for praying. But I'm rusty.

Dear Lord keep them away from Brian's gun. . . . Lord, keep Brian going until his backup gets there, Lord please, God please. Help him. Help him help him.

I feel the tide turning when I hear Brian yell, *"Put your hands on your head! Put your fucking hands on your head!"*

He is only in his thirties. He is screaming like a scared dog and breathing heavily out of his mouth. I don't know him well. I think he's been married a couple of years. I wonder if he'll tell this story to his wife.

Whatever you do, don't think you can understand what it's like to be a cop.

When his backup arrives, I hang up. I unclench. *Thank you, God. Thank you thank you thank you.*

* * *

I'm working as Data Goddess the day that I meet Mona. Data is the channel that cops call in order to find out if the car they're trailing might be stolen or if the male or female they're talking to has any warrants or wants. Some people call it "Data Bitch," but I like to stay positive. I figure if I start the shift as bitch, there's really nowhere to go from there.

Data Goddess (or God, as the case may be) is the person responsible for the infamous "be on the lookout" announcements you always hear in the movies. "White male, five-foot-seven, medium build, blond hair, hates his mother . . ."

I'm finishing up a "missing person" teletype on a teenage runaway, who will most likely be back home the very second I enter her information into the statewide database, when Mona and her entourage breeze into the comm center.

Mona is about six months old. Her mother is a friend of Lily's and her dad is a Roseville Area High School liaison cop (or, as we used to call them in high school, a rent-a-cop). I try not to gawk at babies I've never met, but Lily seems to sense my interest from across the comm center. Before I know it, Lily is propping Mona in a sitting position on my printer and asking me if I want to hold her.

Not really. Well, okay, a little. But just an itsy bitsy wittle minute. . . .

Mona is darling. She is enchanting. She is all the corny things that we say about babies even when they're not any of those things. I stare at Mona's flawless olive skin. I notice the brown eyes and thick lashes she inherited from her dad, Peng. She has her mother Karen's nose and silky hair.

I sit her up on my knees so she can see my face, and I coo to her: "Asian female. Two-foot-two. No bigger than a minute. Big brown eyes! Beautiful brown hair! Armed with a loaded diaper. May need a nappy." I'm being ridiculous, but nobody can hear me and Mona is totally digging it, so I continue: "Wanted for stealing everybody's heart and felony cuteness."

She gazes at my forehead and wraps her chubby little digits around my thumb. She smells like soap and oatmeal. She is magic.

After a few minutes, she begins to fuss, which sets Karen's radar off. She lifts Mona off my lap, takes her in her arms and rests her slightly on her protruding belly. She is five months along.

"She was helping me run data," I tell Karen, as Mona's fingers release my thumb and grab for her mother's necklace.

"Ahh."

We talk about babies for a bit, but it's not a subject I know a lot about, so pretty soon, Mona and Karen are on their way out the door and waving "buh-bye" to their admirers.

I never met Peng's family before.

A couple weeks later, I get a call at Roseville High School: Sixteen-year-old male running in the halls, out of control. Threatened a male teacher with a knife. Unknown where the knife is. Unknown exactly where suspect is.

I enter the call and wait for the lead dispatcher to air

it. Peng is likely already on campus, so he will get the call first and won't have any backup for a few minutes.

I think about Mona, Karen, and Karen's belly.

* * *

Lots of people, especially during medical emergencies, ask us to tell the emergency workers not to use their sirens. This, I assume, is usually an attempt to keep the neighbors from knowing about their business in some form or fashion. Which I do understand.

But my personal policy is that I only tell my medics, fire fighters, and officers where to go and what to expect. I don't tell them how to do their jobs. And anyway, they wouldn't listen if I did. You can't have emergency workers who are fearless and strong and willing to face the unthinkable, yet bend to every little customer-service-oriented whim a citizen may have. It just doesn't work that way.

* * *

Though I never actually worked as a nurse, I imagine that the relationship between cops and dispatchers could be similar to that of doctors and nurses. We make work for them and they make work for us. We try not to, but sometimes they think we don't try hard enough. We feel the same way. We are the middlemen between the cops and the "customers"—the public. It's hard not to get trampled when you're standing between people in crisis and cops who just want to go home at the end of the day.

Some of what we do for the cops is just plain lame.

One night, I get a call from a cop who has arrested a male with a felony warrant from another county about twenty-five miles from ours. He tells me he wants to make a "meet" with that county so they can take their guy to jail. So I give him the number for their county dispatch and hang up. He calls back on the non-emergency line, pissed off.

"Sheriff's Department, this is Caroline."

"Yeah, Gina? Are you the one I just talked to?"

"Yeah," I tell him, a little edgy. Geez, there's only four of us here, and I'm the only newbie, so I figure he knows who he's talking to and is really just being a dink at this point.

"Well, I need *you* to call Hennepin. Call me back and let me know what they say."

I hang up, also pissed.

"Matthews wants me to arrange a meet with Hennepin!" I tell Lisa, sitting next to me on data.

"Well, *yeah*," she says. "It's your *job*."

Oh. What?

So, I arrange the meet, but because there are now *two* middlemen involved (myself and the Hennepin County dispatcher) it takes four phone calls back and forth about who they got, where to meet, what time . . . it's like playing "secretary," only without the slumber party and the fun.

It took me a while to realize all that cops have to deal with out in the real world. They don't have the time or ability to be on the phone for more than a minute or so at a time. And then when they're done dealing with the real world, they have to come back to the station and write a 10-page dissertation about every call they took. No thanks. After I take a call, all I have to do is figure out what page I was on before I threw my book down.

Still, sometimes I get jealous of all that the cops get to *know*. We take all these wild calls that start with screams or cries or silence or even laughter, we try to decipher what's going on for five or ten minutes, then we have to let it go. We don't get to find out if Mr. Brown was having a heart attack or just indigestion. We don't get to know who got arrested at the domestic call, John Doe or Jane Doe. We don't get nearly as many "fuck you's" as the cops do, which means we also almost never get "thank you's."

When I come home after work, Jim often asks about my day. I tell him about this fight or that robbery, and he always wants to know, "Then what?" "Did they catch him?" "Did she get arrested?" "How'd the fire start?"

I almost never know. Finding out would mean hitting up the cops for information every time they walk in the door. Most of them don't have time; some of them don't want to talk about it. You have to economize that kind of thing, so I only ask about the ones I'm really dying to know about. Otherwise, I just read the local newspaper and get half the story like everybody else.

"911?"

Once, when I was living in an apartment with just my cat, Sesame, my best friend came over unexpectedly. She had just bought a new dachshund puppy and was so excited to show him off that when I opened my door to let her in, she let the dog just charge right past me and into big, mean orange Sesame. I had never heard a dog scream with fear. The cat attacked everyone in its sight, including me, but we all lived. When it was all over, we stuffed the smelliest dog on the planet (ever smelled a scared dog?) into her Geo Metro and went downtown for some gourmet pizza. We just sat there, traumatized, chewing on our thin crust, saying, "Man, I can still hear that dog screaming."

What I hear when I pick up this call is worse than that. It's scared human screaming. It is about five seconds before I realize she's actually saying words, but I can't make them out. I start to sweat. I swivel toward my supervisor, my friend.

"Marsha."

Marsha's already been looking my way. The screaming from my phone is filling the room. When she broadcasts the call, the screaming can be heard by the officers listening to Marsha speak on the air.

"2453."

"2453?"

". . . And a squad to back, please. 5444 Willamette Circle on a 911 open line. All we can hear is screaming at this time. Unknown what's wrong. No priors at this address."

I listen to this for another minute or so. I can vaguely make out the woman screaming, "He fell out," but I can't be sure. Then I am disconnected. Nobody answers on the call back.

After a few minutes on scene, our squads call out that they are Code 4.

Code 4 with what?

I will need to know how this story ends. Amazed by the sheer volume of it, Marsha replays the call for everyone in the comm center to hear. I bum a cigarette off Marsha and step outside.

After a few minutes, Steve joins me. I didn't know he smoked. It's also odd because now two of us are out of the comm center at once. I guess that Marsha sent him to see how I'm doing, but it's a role he's not all that comfortable with.

"How's it going?"

"Okay. Just needed a break."

"Yeah?"

"Yeah."

God bless him for trying. I don't even know why I'm so upset, so the idea of explaining it to him is just beyond possibility. It's just that I thought someone was being stabbed to death in my ear for a second there. I just smile and head back in.

I proceed to put an unfair amount of pressure on Marsha to call 2453 and find out what the hell happened on that call. After fourteen years on the job, she is much more familiar with most of the cops than I am. She finally makes the call, which lasts less than a minute. She turns to me with a shrug. "GOA, girly," she says. "Nobody home."

Case closed.

* * *

Got a crush on one of the cops I worked with once. Don't get all excited. What's a crush when you're happily married and not planning to do anything about it? I'm sure he had no idea.

Anyway, I just liked the guy. He was one of the only cops I ever talked to for any length of time, and he looked *great* in uniform, which is the only way I ever saw him. *Truly.*

Well, think what you want.

He touched the back of my neck one day, just to get my attention. I almost dropped to my knees.

Hostages

Rick is the best masseuse, amateur or otherwise, that I've ever known.

"I think my shoulders were taken hostage too," I say in between moans, as Rick works the knots out with short, gentle fingers.

Nobody died, that was the main thing. Nobody got hurt and nobody died. But I can't let it go. I go over and over it. I keep hearing Marsha, saying to no one in particular, and certainly not over the main, "Somebody's going to get shot tonight."

Karaoke is in full swing at the Shoreside Bar. Neither Jim nor I drink, but we go every Wednesday after I get off work, just to talk to Rick and Renae, throw our money away on pull-tabs, and sing country songs. As we order our sodas, a middle-aged pull-tab lady sings "Somewhere Over the Rainbow," lifting her free arm toward the ceiling tiles like she's Judy Garland at Carnegie Hall.

Rick ends the back rub with a friendly squeeze on my shoulder and asks if it helped. I keep my head down for a moment longer, then just nod gratefully.

Nobody shot. Nobody hurt.

On a big screen TV mounted on the wall opposite the bar, Channel 11 relays its version of what happened. There had been a raid on a meth lab at the Motel 6, then a foot chase. When forced to choose between giving up and not, the twenty-two-year-old Michael Robert Somebody-or-other had led police on a foot chase and eventually taken an old man hostage in his own house.

What they don't say is that the suspect entered at least three other houses before he stopped. I had taken the calls. Three intruder calls, one after another.

Did you see a gun? Did he have a weapon? Did he hurt you?

It's all about the gun. The cops need to know about the gun. Knives can get hairy; bats, sticks, whatever. But the gun is the thing that's going to keep somebody—some cop—from going home.

When the first calls started coming in, there were only four of us in the 911 center. Those are the minutes that matter most, yet they're the ones involving the fewest people. If somebody gets shot, it's on our shoulders.

Marsha, in charge of us all, was in the deep pit of hell. Cops were calling out their locations to her over the air, one after another, in rapid succession. There was no way to remember it all and no way to type it. Her backup guy was busy paging the CERT (Community Emergency Response) Team, and Casey and I just kept answering more calls from people who were either watching the chase or had just seen our young suspect in their yards . . . or their kitchens.

"Somebody needs to be typing!" Marsha said to no one in particular.

Somebody's going to get shot tonight.

* * *

Two minutes before all hell breaks loose, I am squirming in my chair like a little kid. I wish Casey would tell somebody when he leaves the room; I have to pee like a racehorse. There have to be at least three of us in here at all times, no matter what. So when he steps out of the room to call his flavor of the week, he should at least announce it. That way I can run to the john first, instead of sitting here with my bladder on fire.

He returns, and I'm on the phone with a medical, of course. "Is that your baby crying?" I ask the twenty-one-year-old mother calling from the Townsedge Terrace trailer park—sorry, mobile home community.

"Yes!"

"Well, it sounds like he's getting air, then. Where's the piece of food he was choking on?"

"I don't know."

"Okay, well the crying is still a good sign. We've got police and medics coming, so just take a deep breath."

"The cops are here!" Mom says excitedly.

"Go let him in," I tell her, then listen to one last sob from the baby, then the click of being let go.

I stand up and face Marsha, who is blowing her nails dry on one hand, casually answering the officers over the main radio channel with the other.

"What up, B?" (That's short for Beautiful.)

"I'm stepping out, G." (Gorgeous.)

Marsha nods at me from behind her mike. Then, from somewhere in Ramsey County, a cop cues a portable packset, and she tilts her head casually toward the speaker, waiting.

"2591!"

"2591?" Marsha replies.

"I've got two at gunpoint at the Six and one running eastbound. I need help here."

All ten of Marsha's newly polished digits clutch her computer hutch as she slams herself upright in front of the monitor.

"Copy. 2591 is out with two at Motel 6. 2591 exactly where are you at Motel 6?"

Nothing.

"2591? 2591?"

"2591, are you Code 4? 2591?" Marsha is like a mother calling her child away from the deep end of a swimming pool, knowing she can't dive in after him if he goes.

She continues: "Any available squads please head to Motel 6 to assist 2591 with two at gunpoint and one suspect running. 20:46."

"2580 . . . Marsha, is our suspect armed?"

"2580, we don't know yet."

Then, as if he had never been away, Marsha's prodigal cop comes back to us.

"2591."

"2591?" Marsha says, holding the cross around her neck in one hand, keying her mike with the other.

"I'm Code 4 for now. And both my parties were armed. I don't know about the runner."

"2580 do you copy?"

" '80 copies."

"2591 is Code 4 at 20:47."

"Jesus Christ," Marsha says, leaning back. It's not a curse, but maybe a prayer. Or just a statement.

About an hour and a half later, when Mike puts his hand on my shoulder and asks if I need a break, I remember about having to pee. By this time, everyone and his mother is in the dispatch center. Steve had pretty much paged out the whole department, and within thirty minutes, the place more closely resembles a retirement shindig than a crisis center. There's pizza. There's coffee. There are doughnuts and supervisors.

I don't know what my body did with my water, and it takes me a minute to realize that all my muscles have been in contraction for a little over ninety minutes.

"Jesus." I stutter. "Yeah. I . . ." I realize Mike doesn't need the details of the stress my bladder has been through, so I stop talking.

Nobody shot yet. Take a deep breath.

* * *

The old man is still in the house with the young guy, and we still don't know about a gun. But the wife of the hostage says there are guns in the house. That's the main thing now. That and fielding calls from what seems like just about every last one of Roseville's population of thirty-something-thousand, asking what's the deal with the thirty-odd squad cars on and around Rose Place.

"Do we need to be concerned?"

Be afraid. Be very afraid.

"No, ma'am. We have a contained hostage situation," I tell her. I never imagined that I would talk like a cop, but there I am, spewing all this cop-talk under pressure. "No, ma'am, there's no danger for you unless you're in that house."

"Oh, my."

Oh my, indeed.

* * *

About 22:35, Michael Robert Nobody, white male, age twenty-two, leaves the old man's house with his hands way, way up, and all of his hostages start to release themselves from him. But some of us take longer than others.

When Marsha hugs me at the end of my shift, I feel the rock-hard tension in my shoulders. I see the weight of that whole night in her face. She had been the one the cops had called with their packsets halfway down their throats, telling her things she couldn't always comprehend and giving her locations that may or may not have made sense. But you can't not know when you're sitting in her chair.

Does Prior Avenue even cross Rose Place? Where's 2580? Have we heard from him? Is there a gun? Does anyone know about the gun? Godammit.

If someone had gotten shot, the bullet would have gone right through her.

"Good job, B. Love you."

"You, too."

"You going home?"

"Going to karaoke."

When I get to the Shoreside, Rick and Renae and Jim are all waiting to hear my exciting story, the story of what made me so late. I tell them what I can remember.

I tell the story of worst night of an old man's life over the blare of a white forty-something woman singing, *"All my exes live in Texas. . . ."*

I tell them the pieces I have made peace with. The rest I leave in my shoulders and my heart. Don't know where else it can really go.

"Hey," Rick says, rolling up his sleeves. It seems my shoulders were calling to him, *Help me.* "Put your head down like this," he tells me, "Now put your arms way up."

Smucked

It's kind of a shock for me, the first time I hear someone make light of death. A man has been hit on the freeway by a semi and killed instantly. I overhear the night shift supervisor, Anne, tell someone, "He got smucked."

What an awful thing to say. I look around to see if anyone else is as shocked as I am. Nope. I wonder if I will be like that someday too, someone with no respect for the dead.

As the details start to trickle in, we learn that the guy had been drunk, and he had been hit while running from the scene of an accident with injuries—which he had caused. When it came time to peel the man's dead body from various locations on the freeway, several of the cops at the scene recognized his photo ID as someone they had met many times before.

I pull up his apprehension sheet on the county database. His past is littered with DWIs and DWI-related charges. Also listed are his past warrants. Failure to appear for domestic assault. Failure to appear for felony terroristic threats. Narcotics. Felony theft.

On the police report, he will be called the victim. But there are other victims involved. They are the truck driver, who now has to live with the idea that he ran a man over. There are the injured people in the other car at the scene of the hit-and-run. And last, but not least, there are the medical workers, firefighters, and cops who had to show up and see what they saw. They had to bag up the body parts, take pictures, and wash blood off the road.

Maybe it's not about respect for the dead. It's about picking which baggage is worth carrying with you later, when you go out into the real world, where people don't want to hear about body parts on the road. Most likely, *someone* will mourn for the guy who got smucked on the freeway. It just might not be Anne . . . or me.

On the Night Shift

Though I don't get to work it very much, I like night shift the best.

Day shift is full of the things you never realized you signed up for when you took the job. Day shift is when people call to complain about the stop sign at the corner of Fifth and Dakota and how nobody stops for it and why don't we have a cop sit there all day and write tickets? Day shift and afternoon shift are when someone has a fender-bender in rush-hour traffic and twenty-one different people use twenty-one different cell phones to call us on twenty-one different lines to tell us about the same accident.

Afternoon shift is when all the families of the world sit down to dinner in their respective homes and 99.9 percent get along just swell and the other .1 percent have to call us to break up whatever domestic situation has gotten underway. Afternoon shift, in the summer, is also when the heat starts to make people crazy, and they do things maybe they wouldn't normally do, like rob banks or drink too much warm beer.

Night shift is about real emergencies or nothing at all. Nobody calls you at 3:15 AM to report their dog missing or to complain about their neighbor's sprinkler hitting their house, and *almost* nobody wants to debate the validity of a traffic ticket at 3:15 AM.

One Tuesday night, for at least an hour, not a single call comes in at all. I sit next to Kendra, a married lady with two boys ages twelve and nine and a new puppy who chews everything in the house and still gets displayed prominently in three big pictures on her locker. When we start blabbing, it's about the upcoming presidential election. She wants George W. to pick Condi Rice for a running mate and win a landslide victory. I want George W. to pick Hillary for a running mate, then I want him to take a long walk off a short pier. We agree to disagree.

She tells me about her sister, who lives out East. Book smart, but stupid in love. She tells me about her husband, who works afternoon shift at some place that doesn't need to be open that late in her opinion, and her boys, whose amateur hockey careers are putting them all in the poorhouse.

At some point, Lily, who is sitting across from us on the main, gives us some grief about all the yakking, calls us Chatty Cathys. She has been quietly reading a book about raising confident girls. Some day soon, Lily will fly to India to adopt a two-year-old girl, whose name is Ranjana. She and her husband have been waiting for months to get word about when this will take place. It's useless to try to understand why they must wait so long. We have all been staring at the same two pictures of the little girl for months. The first picture Lily got is taped to her locker, and has since been made into the wallpaper on the main computer. Little Ranjana stares out at us from the screen in mismatched clothing, pulled too high at the waist. She looks tired but anxious, like her mom in America.

Ranjana's third birthday is coming up in the fall, and Lily worries that she might not be able to celebrate it with her. She gets letters from the orphanage, updating her on her daughter's life. Ranjana has contracted some sort of pox from other kids in the orphanage, they tell her. She is shy and small for her age.

I am getting ready to adopt as well. Lucy's mother has given me permission to adopt her, and the paperwork is underway. Because Lucy already lives with us, the process will be quick and painless. In watching Lily, I have begun to see how lucky I am. Whether Lucy is "mine" on paper yet or not, and even whether I feel like a true mother or not, at least I have her with me.

In my prayers, I ask God to make Lily and me complete mothers, with children, and signed and stamped paperwork, and tears and joy. I also pray that Lucy doesn't put me through *any* of the crap I put my own mother through. But I know that if she does, I'll stand by her. Just like my mother did.

Sometimes I wonder: How does God handle all the 911 calls that He gets?

I stand up to stretch, then just stand there and make

faces at Lily until she looks at me. She sticks her tongue out back at me. Then she gets on the building intercom and says to a whole two floors' worth of empty rooms:

"Will my breakfast burrito please report to the comm center? Will my breakfast burrito *please* report to the comm center."

Sometimes this actually works and some deputy takes pity on us and brings us food. It doesn't have to be a breakfast burrito, per se. Anything that can't be sold in a vending machine is fine.

One 911 line rings, and it's like a car alarm bleating out into our quiet comm center air. I punch the blinking line. I have to be quick to beat the two other ladies.

"911?"

"I want someone to come out here and look at what my neighbor is doing to me."

"You live in the Rose Vista apartments, Number 485?"

"Yes."

"What is your neighbor doing?"

"She waits for me to leave, then she comes in here and pees in my laundry basket."

"She what?"

"She pees in the basket in my closet. She thinks I don't know it's her. But I *know*."

"Is she there now?"

"No! She thinks I don't know about her, but I know."

If there's one thing I've learned about knowing things, it's that nobody knows anything, and it's only the crazy people of the world who know that they know. And it's usually only the crazy people who like to call us at 3:25 AM and tell us what they know that they know.

"Is your name Eleanor?"

"Yes. How did you know that?"

"It's on my computer screen." Ah, *geez*. Now she's going to think I'm the invisible 911 operator who broke in last week and pooped in her breakfast cereal.

I keep Eleanor on the line until I hear the cops knocking at her door.

"Oh!" she exclaims at the sound of them. "They're here!" It's as if she's the host at a Christmas cocktail party, and her first guests have finally arrived. She disconnects before we even have a chance to say proper good-byes.

"Where were we?" I turn back to Kendra, who is cutting cheese slices to go with her plate of sliced apples.

"Oh," she recalls cheerfully, "I was telling you about the time I . . ."

I don't know how we got on the subject, but it's now close to 4:00 AM and Kendra has begun telling me about the time she drove herself to the hospital, thinking she had the flu. She begins to describe, in detail, how her condition worsened along the way.

She threw up. Then there was blood when she threw up. On her way to the hospital, she brought an empty Kemps ice cream bucket to deposit the vomit into, which was filling more and more with blood. Then she got to the emergency room and apparently didn't faze any of the nurses with her bucket o' blood and was told to sit down and wait while she continued to brack.

I begin to picture this in my head. I'm getting woozy.

In my attempts to lose weight, or to at least not get any fatter, I haven't eaten too much on this night. What's more, I'm a ninny who grosses out easily. I thought I was past all that, but I'm not. And I don't want to admit this to two women who, as far as I can tell, possess stomachs of cast iron.

There's no blood. It's just a story. I'm a 911 operator. It's my job to listen to stories, often disgusting ones. I should be able to hear about Kendra's puke-fest without puking myself.

My ears start to ring. I'm going to faint.

Apparently, a nice young black man in the emergency room literally picked Kendra up in his arms and demanded that she be attended to, and then she was. I can't hear the rest over the bells in my head. It doesn't matter that Kendra's about to get help from the good doctors and nurses in her story. Or that she's sitting in front of me now, healthy and whole. I've been grossed out, and it appears there's no turning back.

I say something lame about the bathroom and make a beeline for the door. I make it down the hall, through the two sets of doors, and to the toilet stall without fainting.

I like this stall. It has become a refuge for me in difficult times. The bathroom tile is cold and earth-toned, and like the comm center, it almost never gets a meaningful cleaning. There is a sign above the stool reminding me not to flush the handle with my foot, or I might break something. Other than that, there is no "communication." There are no radios and no phones in the bathroom stall.

I have stared at this cold tile floor many times. Sometimes after a suicidal. Sometimes after I make a big huge mistake. Sometimes after doing everything right and watching everything go to hell anyway. Sometimes because I actually have to pee.

I wait for the ringing to pass. I know from experience, from nursing school, from all the things that have passed before, that eventually, this too will pass. I pray the Hail Mary, though I am not Catholic. I choose it because it's one that I can remember. The ringing subsides.

Eventually, I slink back in to the comm center and plant myself at my console. If Kendra knows anything about what just happened, she doesn't let on. I don't volunteer it, either. Instead, I sit quietly for a while and chew on my chocolate-frosted Zingers from the vending machine.

When the shift ends for us at about 6:50 AM, Kendra says something about how much fun it was talking to me all night.

It was. I agree, and I mean it.

* * *

The following is taken from a taped recording of a night shift call. I didn't take it, but I think both the caller and the operator deserve the recognition.

"911?"

"Is there anybody there who's in charge of the office that I can talk to?"

"In charge of what office?"

"Well, you're the dispatcher?"

"Mmmhmm."

"Well, I don't know if this is really a dispatching idea, but . . ."

"Okay, I need you to tell me what . . ."

"Okay, here's what it is. I just talked to the Secret Service and I told them that I think that if we had a pig lift-and-drop in Baghdad that the enemy would retreat. They are deathly afraid of pig blood. See, they're not going to put any suicide bombers out there. They're going to be trapped in their underground bunkers, and we don't have to go in and that type of thing. Now, we thought about dropping pig blood on Afghanistan, but evidently they decided against it. Thought they'd do it conventionally, and not offend anybody. But I think things are getting out of hand. And we don't have to worry so much about offending if we put in a live pig. And, of course, Ventura got the pig market under control, he tried to sell it to China and Cuba. He knows where the pigs are."

Our caller sounds like a white female, possibly in her sixties or seventies. No, she is not messing with us. And yes, it is entirely possible that our esteemed former governor does indeed know where the pigs are.

"Okay, now the reason I'm running this by you is that I think that the pigs could be a deterrent under the Homeland Security. Because, you know, we've relied on our German shepherd dogs, and I'm not suggesting that the police have a pig on a leash"—because that, apparently, would be crazy—"but a pig in the back yard isn't so bad. If you give them hydrogen peroxide in the water, they don't stink, see. And a lot of people have pigs for pets. So it could be a pig for a pet. For the Homeland Security issue. If you want to run that by 'em, that would be fine."

"Okay, yeah, I can do that, okay? But that's more of a military issue, though. The sheriff's department has nothing to do with Baghdad."

"But the police are responsible for Homeland Security, and that's too much."

"Yeah . . ."

"See? They need the cooperation of the homeowner. Now homeowners interested in having a pig for a pet, and giving them hydrogen peroxide in the water so they don't stink, and dispose of their feces, well, they're not any more trouble than a dog!"

Eureka!

"Yeah, that's something that you'd probably want to direct somewhere else." Like a licensed therapist. "I don't think the sheriff's department is interested in pigs."

"What I'm trying to tell you is that terrorism on the home front could be relieved to a great extent . . . I mean, I can't very well have a pig because I have two dogs."

Wait a minute. All this and she's not going to do her part for homeland security?

"Yeah, I can't have a pig either."

She laughs. "But there are people that can! It would be nice. It would be a deterrent."

"Yeah, okay. Well, I'll run it by my sergeant, okay, and see what he says."

"Okay, yeah, pass it along."

"Okay, thank you."

"Okay, bye."

Okay, then.

* * *

I give a tour to a small group of Boy Scouts who are visiting the sheriff's department. Apparently, these boys have yet to earn their "personal space" badges, because they absolutely swarm me the entire time. Several of them commit the cardinal sin of dispatch and touch the receiver on my phone. When you work as closely with your partners as I do, you become concerned—okay, *obsessive*—about germs. I sanitize my phone at the beginning of every shift. If I didn't, I would be sick once a month. I make a mental note to re-sanitize after they leave.

I try to explain the job to them, but all they really want to know is if I get to play computer games when I get bored.

At that point, a little nub of a man, who I can only assume is the Scout leader, interrupts my answer and firmly tells his strangely-odored little boy cubs that there is never a reason to be bored and that boredom is only a state of mind. So, there you go. A little bit of life advice from a grown man wearing a red kerchief around his neck.

Sit in my shoes at 0300 hours on a Wednesday morning, just clinging to consciousness while the rest of the world is asleep (or dead, but not discovered yet), then come talk to me about your state of mind.

Maybe you've been on duty since 1900 the previous day, and you've handled two armed robbery calls, three domestics, and a house fire already. You know there's more coming, but you don't know when. You could sit and worry about what it will be, or you could just be bored.

Once, I even fall asleep on night shift. When I wake up, I have a phone to my ear, and a woman who has just found her husband dead on the bathroom floor.

How's that for state of mind?

That Loving Feeling

"Nine . . ."

Click.

The phone disconnects before I can say all three numbers. When I call back, a young woman answers. She is out of breath, and there is a baby wailing in the background.

"This is the sheriff's department. Is everything okay?"

"Um, I just wanted him to leave, that's all."

"What happened?"

"He hit me in the head and slammed me up against the wall."

"Is he still there? Why did you hang up?"

"He's still here, but he took the phone away from me when I tried to call."

Misdemeanor domestic assault, plus gross misdemeanor 911 interference, equals at least a night or two in the penalty box. I take a minute to type her name and some other info into the system, then listen to make sure Kristen has gotten the squads going. In the short time that takes, I have lost my caller's attention.

As I listen, the two lovers argue back and forth about whether he really hit her. Then it turns quiet, except for the baby.

"Jamie? Jamie, what's going on?"

"Don't," she says, not to me.

The man's voice says, "I'm going to do it. It's time for me to die."

"Don't," she begs him.

"Jamie, what does he have?"

A gun? A knife? A bomb? What?

"It's time," he says again. "It's time for me to die."

The baby wails and begins to sound out of breath. I've never taken care of an infant for any length of time. I wonder what she needs, and wish I could give it to her. Is she hungry? Is she scared? Shouldn't Mom go and hold her now?

After about one minute of this, I begin to realize what Jamie does not: That dipshit *isn't* going to kill himself. He just wants her to think that he will.

To guys like him, women are necessary for survival. She is a roof over his head and a bed and a body to curl up with at night. He will be as sorry and as suicidal as he needs to be to make sure that he still has her waiting when he pleads guilty to disorderly conduct in front of a disinterested judge, then gets released from jail.

So he keeps it up. Later I learn he was holding a knife to his throat. Must have seen that in a movie or something. Judging by the way she is eating his little act with a spoon, I assume he had no trouble going right back to Jamie's apartment the next day. That's what guys like him live on, women who buy their stupid crap.

I would love to get him on the phone and tell him to go ahead and do it. I know he won't. But I'd love to say, "Go ahead and do it, worm. You don't have the guts."

I guess this is another case of free will I'm just going to have to get used to. He's a shithead. I can't change it. And she's making her choices. I can't change her. I only have her for these few minutes to do anything to help. He's a big boy and she's a big girl.

But when I hang up on Jamie and the cops call a Code 4, one in custody, it's not the man's raspy voice or Jamie's pleas that ring in my ears.

It's the baby's cries.

* * *

I know exactly what a punch sounds like over the phone, or a slap. But I don't know if I could identify the sound if it happened right in front of my face.

* * *

We get a lot of domestics. One of the cops I work with likes to say, "Yeah, they lost that loving feeling. I hate it when that happens."

"911?"

"Get off me! Get away from me! Motherfucker, I'll fuckin' kill you if you don't get away from me."

"Ma'am?"

"You gotta send someone over here because he's got to go."

"Is he your boyfriend?"

"Hell no!"

"Ex-boyfriend?"

"Yeah."

I can see why, especially at this moment, my caller would want to make the distinction: She doesn't want to be reminded that she ever tried to share a life with him. But from a law enforcement standpoint, it's all the same. Husband, ex-husband, fiancé, ex-fiancé . . . doesn't matter. Whatever the case, it's one or both people in a relationship who just don't know when to say "good-bye"—or at least "good night."

"I'm on the lease. You can't tell me to leave," comes the other side of the story from somewhere in the room.

"Ma'am, did he hit you tonight?" I have learned to say *tonight* because that's all we need to know about *for now.* If I'm not careful, I could get the history of the whole relationship, which I don't have time for.

"Naw, but he's throwing things around and talkin' shit."

"Has anyone been drinking?"

"He's been drinking all day."

"Bullshit! Well, if I have, then so have you!"

Ah, the old "two drunks make a right" defense.

"I had two beers," my female yells at us both.

I mute my line. "They're both D-K," I tell Lily, who is dispatching the call on the main. Another odd cop-ism I never thought I'd use.

"Any weapons?" Lily's eyebrows go up.

"Do either of you have any weapons?" I ask. "Ma'am?"

Sometimes I hesitate to ask about weapons because more often than not, the question plants an idea. For example: "Are there any weapons in the house, ma'am?" Caller: "No . . . well, I guess there's the butcher knife. Or I guess there's Billy's baseball bat in the corner. . . . Yeah! Yeah, there are plenty of weapons I could use!"

I repeat the question about weapons, but nobody's listening to me now. From what I can tell, my caller and her *ex*-boyfriend, with whom she lives and spent the day drinking, have returned to hashing out their differences in the only way they know: screaming at the top of their lungs.

All I can do now is listen. It matters what happens during these minutes before the officers arrive. Maybe he will hit her and I will hear the thud of it. Maybe she will throw something. Maybe he will yank the phone out of the wall. Maybe someone will take out a knife or a gun. This doesn't often happen, but I need to know if it does, which is why I'll stay on the line until I hear the cop call a "Code 4" on the main.

When my ex-couple hears a knock at the door, they stop yelling long enough to let the officer in. When he asks them what's going on, they tell him, and tell him and tell him.

Two people in the middle of hating each other who used to love each other can say the darndest things. I once heard a woman tell her husband (on my recorded line) that he smoked way more crack than she did.

When I've got two people who want to kill each other on the line, I try to get the more aggressive one on the phone with me. That way, he or she can direct all complaints, claims of wrongdoing, cursing, and screaming at the Complaints Department (me). And if the aggressor is focused on me, he or she is no longer stabbing the other party in the eye, throwing a lamp across the room, or whatever was going on before I got involved.

Sometimes this backfires and I get both parties on two different extensions yelling at me about their sex lives, their overdue mortgage, his gambling problem, her cheating on him, and anything else they want to share. And in this age of cordless phones, sometimes my callers are able to multitask: screaming at me on the phone *while* trying to kill each other. I'm waiting for the day when someone puts me on speaker phone so as to keep *both hands* free to strangle a spouse.

Lily says that everyone, when new to the job, tries to be a social worker. I did, too. I had been going to Alcoholics Anonymous for ten years, and I had tools for dealing with dysfunction. I *knew stuff.*

In the heat of a rip-roaring domestic, I might say something like, "Ma'am, just let it go," or "Sir, maybe you should take a look at your drinking, since it's only 9:45 AM and you've already had a six-pack." Or my personal favorite: After my caller said she had been told she was a less skilled lover than her husband's new girlfriend, I asked, gently, "How does that make you feel?"

The problem is that while I was trying to play Dr. Phil, I was forgetting to get the basics. Are there any injuries? Anyone like to beat up cops over there? Anyone been drinking or getting high? I learned slowly that it's not my job to say all the healing things that I like to hear myself say. It's my job to get a picture of the scene and let the officer say all the things that should be said, which will also likely fall on deaf ears, but at least it will be done once everyone is safe. For now.

I'm sure it's true what most cops say: that domestics

are the most dangerous calls that they take. The only danger we dispatchers face is that we might get too sucked in. I take each call very seriously, but I try not to crawl inside. I've been there, done that. I don't need to stay.

I remind myself frequently: Most people don't treat each other that way.

And even though I'll never know how it ends for these people who call, sometimes I imagine what their lives would be like after a little bit of growth. Sounds silly, but it makes me feel better. Like, maybe my female caller later moved back to her mom's house and enrolled in school. Maybe the male got court-ordered into alcohol treatment and it changed his life. It could happen. Growth happens all the time. Good things happen, I remind myself often. It's just that nobody calls 911 to tell us about it when it does.

Just Too Silly

"911?"

"I live in North Oaks. There's someone trying to get into my house."

North Oaks is the only gated community in our county, and the average home price is about double or triple what we paid for our house. Most callers let us know that they're from North Oaks right up front, so we can make sure we're giving the level of service that they are accustomed to.

"You're at 455 Highfield Street?"

"Yes."

"An intruder to your house?"

"He's at the back door."

"Do you know who he is?"

"No! He tried to turn the knob, and when he couldn't get in, he started banging on the door. Now he's out there laughing at me."

"He's laughing?"

"Yes."

"Does he have any weapons?"

"I don't think so. I don't know. Oh, hurry."

"And you've never seen him before?"

"No!"

Lily dispatches the call to two of our deputies. I keep my caller on the line while she waits for them.

"Oh, God, hurry!"

"We've got two squads on the way. What's your name?"

"My name is Wanda Everton. I'm a lawyer. I shouldn't be this hysterical."

"It's okay, just take a deep breath. What's he doing now? Can you still see him?"

"No."

I'm about to get a description when I see that Casey is snapping his fingers at me for attention.

"I've got your intruder on the line."

"Huh?"

"Your guy at the back door. Line 3. He says he's her lawn guy."

"You're crapping me."

"Negative. He just wanted a phone book so he could call a cab."

Ah, *geez.*

"Wanda? Are you still there?"

"Yes!"

"Did you have your lawn done today?"

"I guess so, why?"

"Your intruder is on hold with us. He's your lawn guy."

"What? . . . Oh my God, I'm so embarrassed. Oh my. Uh, am I going to get charged for this?"

"No. Better safe than sorry, right?"

"Oh my God, I'm an idiot. I'll go get him that phone book."

"Okey-doke. Bye, now."

* * *

Once I took a call in which an Asian male in his twenties walked up to the clerk at a movie theater and asked her for a pen and some paper. She obliged him, and he then sat down in the lobby and scribbled something down.

When she saw him again, he was in her face with the paper she gave him, which said something like, "Give me all the money. I have a gun."

He got some money and left on foot. We never caught him.

Once, one of my partners took a call in which a white male walked up to the clerk at a fast-food restaurant and told her to put all the money in this paper sack he handed her. When asked if he showed her the gun, she said "No." In fact, he never said he had a gun, or anything. He just wanted the money. He got some.

And he got away.

* * *

We get a lot of calls from people who want us to send the fire department to help a cat out of a tree. Some departments will actually start up the cherry picker, suit up, and rescue the little bugger, as it does its feline best to scratch the poor firefighter's eyes out.

Not our departments. We have one standard answer to the caller who asks us to come out and save Fluffy: "Have you ever seen a dead cat in a tree?"

* * *

Ran a personalized plate for an officer once: "POT-MAN." No kidding. I guess "PUL ME OVR" was taken. And "PROBABL CAUS" has too many letters.

* * *

"911?"

"Hi, my name is Duncan Peters and I want to talk to a cop."

"What do you need tonight?"

"Well, everybody thinks I hit my girlfriend and they called the cops and I ran because I was scared, but I didn't hit her."

"Where was this?"

"At her house. Jenkins Street."

When I check Peters's name in our warrants database, I see that he has a felony warrant for walking away from a minimum security workhouse in the county next door. So, really, the whole "who hit who" issue is, well, moot.

I stare at his mug shot on my computer screen. Your average-looking twenty-something guy with short hair and a goatee. Can it be he doesn't remember he's a fugitive?

"Where are you now? I can send someone to talk to you."

"And they're going to listen to my side of the story?"

"Absolutely."

"What did my girlfriend tell them, anyway?"

"I wasn't there, but I'm sure it speaks well for you that you're willing to talk to police about it now, right?"

"Okay, good. Okay. Well, I'm at 2554 Seventh Street."

"Great! We'll be with you shortly."

* * *

A man called one night, wishing to relay a tip that some of his old friends were selling dope out of a local motel. Our tipster then said he wanted to remain "unanimous."

I imagine if he was ever asked to testify on this matter, he would have to assert his Fifth Commandment rights.

Changes

Jogging a couple of miles away from my house, I pass a man who is fumbling around with somebody's garbage can at the end of a driveway. He is so unsteady on his feet that he rolls over right in front of me. He refuses my offer of help, but I figure whatever his problem is, I should have somebody check on him.

I don't have a phone, so I flag down a man in a recycling truck. When I tell him why I need his phone, he refuses me, saying, "If he's still there an hour from now, I'll call police myself."

"But I think he needs help now," I tell him. He hesitates for a second, then again refuses to give me his phone.

I jog a couple of blocks to the county beach. The

teenage lifeguard on her tall white perch tells me she doesn't have a phone (which I find a little odd), but a woman who is watching her children swim offers hers. As I describe the man to the dispatcher, I hear the cell-phone lady say, "Yeah, I saw that guy. I kinda wondered what was wrong with him."

She *wondered*, but she didn't call. It's not unusual for someone to call 911 because some kid stole change from the ash tray of his or her car. But some guy falls over on the street for no known reason, and suddenly we're worried about making an unnecessary call. Why are we so hesitant to act on anyone's behalf but our own?

Maybe I would have ignored drunk garbage guy three years ago. But now? No way.

Lily gave me some good advice about being too timid to act while on the job. A time will come, she told me, when you'll be too shy to clarify something or too intimidated to ask a question that you need to ask, and because you didn't, somebody gets hurt. Maybe somebody gets killed. Then you never make that mistake again.

* * *

I am sensing changes in myself. Some good, some—I don't know. For one thing, people don't bully me nearly as much as they used to before I took this job.

I notice it when I am selling my old Ford. Brad, a dapper-looking middle-aged man, and his son, who never introduces himself, saw the newspaper ad and came to look at it.

As soon as Brad decides he wants the car for his son, he starts this hard-nosed asshole act, which I'm guessing he saves only for vehicle and home purchases and close members of his family. He quotes me a ridiculously low price, and when I refuse it, he starts railing on and on about the blue book and the loan value and how he would rather just walk away than deal with someone who wasn't going to be reasonable.

At which point, I nod, look him in the eye, and say, "And that's your choice."

There was a time when Brad would have gotten me all upset. But I know all about choice now. I listen to people make good and bad choices all day long. If you want to dress up like Nixon and dance around making quote marks in the air, that's your choice. If you want to jump on top of my car and scream like a little girl, again, your choice. Don't care. What's your emergency?

He looks at me like I have just called his mother a whore, but he continues to badger me about my car for a little longer. Perhaps in the past, this bizarre schtick had got Brad what he wanted. But I get yelled at a lot. My supervisor doesn't like how I handle my calls. My callers think the world is ending and that I'm not doing enough to stop it. The cops think I'm too slow, then sometimes too fast. And there's always something more critical than the critical thing I'm dealing with at the moment.

Not only is there no way to make *everyone* happy, it's nearly impossible to make *anyone* happy. And anyway, most people only *think* they want to be happy. Including me. There's something wildly freeing about knowing that.

Two years ago, I might have gone into the ring with mad old Brad. But that was back when I cared about every little blessed thing. When he stomps back to his car and leaves with his young son (who actually looks like he wants the car) in tow, I wave bye-bye like me and Brad are old friends.

Two days later, I sell the car for a little below my asking price to a nice lady from one county over.

Words

The problem with my new takeno-shit attitude is that it makes me a less patient, less sensitive human being. I notice that I have not only less tolerance for bullshit, but also a much wider definition of bullshit than ever before.

When I ask a question, I will tolerate nothing but *the answer.* Anything more or less is simply not acceptable. I get short with people when things get too busy. I can't spend three minutes explaining why someone needs to report a crime in another jurisdiction. I can't go into every detail as to how screwed you are when someone steals your identity and uses your good credit to buy video games. The phones are ringing, I gotta go. Gotta get to the next call.

Because of that, sometimes I find myself taking a certain tone with people that I know I would *hate* if I were on the other end of it.

"Ma'am, I have to ask you to hold. I know you've already been holding. There's nothing I can do about it."

"Sir, there's nothing we can do about your son unless we catch him with drugs on him. He's an adult, and he can stay out all night with drug dealers if he wants to."

It often feels like there's more that we *can't* do than what we *can* do to help people. And because, so often, our job is to get the quick synopsis of whatever's going on, and getting that synopsis can be a life or death thing, it's hard not to let that spill over into the other areas of life.

"Hi, honey, how was school?"

"Well, Brittany told Ashley that I talk too much and I heard her say it, so I said, 'Why don't you just say it to my face,' and she was all, 'Why don't you mind your own business,' and I was like . . ."

"Good or bad! Good or bad and whether or not you're going to live. That's all I want to know."

"Um . . ."

"Do you have any homework?"

"Well, I guess you could say I've got a little, but it's not due until . . ."

"Child! Don't make me hurt you. Yes or no?"

It's like in the old *Dragnet* reruns: just the facts, ma'am, just the facts. I seem to have absolutely no room in my head for extra words. I went from being an editor of written words to an editor of all words. And I can only tolerate so many words in one day's time. I am starting to find my inner Kristen.

Sales people and telemarketers put me through the roof with all their words. Just tell me why you're calling so I can tell you why I don't want what you're selling. And if you're knocking on my door trying to sell me soap, a vacuum, your religion, or anything else I didn't ask to hear about, be prepared to get my door in your face.

What's the rush? Where's the fire? I don't know, but I won't be ready for it with someone yakkin' in my face and wasting my time.

The flip side of that is how I am when it comes to talking to callers during emergencies. The caretaker in me kicks in. If you need me to *save* you, I have all the time it takes. But you have to be careful with that mentality. If your loved ones only get your attention when they are in crisis, pretty soon you've got a lot of crises on your hands, especially with kids. Sometimes I have to remind myself to slow down. My callers are in my life for a few minutes. My loved ones are in my life forever, I hope.

Sometimes I just have to remind myself to save some extra words for them.

Every once in a while, I slow down enough to just talk to people. That's my favorite thing about down time. Dispatchers need those times when we can just yammer on for half an hour with someone who needs it.

Higher-ups and management don't like to hear about down time. It's the old "Time to lean is time to clean!" mentality. But the down time is necessary to make the chaos easier to swallow. And the constant possibility of chaos is what detracts from any time ever truly being *down time*.

I heard a cop say this once: "Sometimes we get paid

not for what we're doing, but for what we could be called upon to do."

Down time does happen. Often, it's on Sundays, or on the night shift, and sometimes in the winter, when it's too cold to go out and rob the liquor store or get into an argument with your husband in the grocery store parking lot. We get to give people the attention they deserve.

It doesn't mean that law enforcement in general can be more helpful on those lazy days, it just means that I have time to tell you why and help you understand. Maybe law enforcement can't help you with that problem, but I give a shit and I'll sit here and listen to your story. I sympathize.

"Yes, ma'am, it stinks that someone is out there trying to use your name to open credit card accounts. I know you must be frustrated."

"Yes, sir. I'm sorry about your son. You must be very scared for him."

Sometimes, that's all a person needs. To be validated, for once. Or to validate.

I also value those days because I get to save more words for my darlings, my chatterbox husband and daughter. Those are the days when it's easy to love them for all their words. And to listen.

On Burnout

Thank you for calling 911. All operators are busy with people who generally try not to live in constant drama, but who need police assistance. To expedite your emergency, please choose from the following options:

If you lent your car to your sister's boyfriend's cousin, who just got out of jail, and whose last name you don't know, and you want to report it stolen, please press 1.

If you are fighting with your baby's daddy, against whom you currently have a restraining order, and with whom you are currently living, please press 2.

If you would like us to raise your children for you, please press 3.

For all alcohol- or drug-related injuries, fallouts, or general debacles, please press 4.

If you would like to report that the guy you "borrowed" $200 to has not returned to "pay you back," then please leave your name, address, and a brief physical description of yourself at the tone.

Thank you for calling your local police, and have a safe and sober day.

* * *

One of my coworkers says sometimes she imagines all the negativity that we encounter on this job as a sort of vapor coming out of the phone, as in a cartoon. I envision the word-cloud on an animated page, and the words "bad juju" written inside it.

Sometimes, I sit in the comm center and forget that I am in the helping business. It's easy to do. Some days it's because I don't like helping people. Some days it's because people don't seem to want to be helped.

The first thing we always ask in an emergency is, "Where are you?" Often, callers don't know.

Always know where you are. I mean, what street are you on? What's the house number? That sort of thing. If you call me on your cell phone, and you don't know where you are, we could have a problem.

There is technology available that can help locate a caller quite easily, but never assume that your local police department is equipped with it. In most jurisdictions, every dime that gets spent on law enforcement is a product of fifteen different advisory board and county board meetings, and by the time it's spent, the technology it bought is obsolete. Or by the time the money is approved to be spent, it's been allocated for some other purpose.

Sometimes, even though you're calling on 911, all an operator can tell for sure is what tower the cell phone signal is bouncing off. That's not enough to find you. When you're out walking or shopping, take the time to notice what street you're on, what store you're at. Many people who call don't even know what city they are in.

The second thing we need to know in an emergency is what's going on. That's a tricky one too. Callers often want help, but not enough to tell me exactly what with.

Often, I struggle to understand why people tell me the things they tell me, as well as why they won't tell me the things they won't. I once had to tell a woman, as she stood there holding the knife her husband just used to stab her son, that I wasn't nearly as interested in her stories of things that happened two months ago as I was in what was happening *at that moment.*

"They used to be good friends!" she told me wistfully. Meanwhile, her wounded, bleeding son was trying to get into his car and drive away. I've got the victim fleeing in his car and the suspect sitting back down in his La-Z-Boy. I need some damn information.

"Which way is he going, ma'am?"

"I don't know. Why do you need to know that?"

Oh, no reason. It's best if you just tell me some more information that I can use, like what's his favorite color, or whether he wears boxers or briefs.

Maybe when you live in constant drama, as this woman did, you tend to get stuck on the details. If I tell them the detail that my husband is a churchgoing, kind-hearted man, then maybe the big detail that he stabbed my son will get overlooked.

More often than not, people in the most volatile situations are the ones offering the least information.

"My husband just pulled a gun on me." Click.

That's it? I'm going to send a bunch of cops—who also happen to be my friends now—and all I get to tell them is, "There's a gun in there. Uhm. Be careful. God bless."

Where's the gun?

Where's the guy?

Who are you?

Who is he?

It seems the more questions we ask, the more irritated callers become. There's never enough time to explain why we ask what we ask. If there was time we would explain it this way: *We are sending help. But the helpers we are sending are human, too. They want some information before they go marching gallantly into harm's way. They all want to go home tonight.*

"911?"

"Someone stole my car!"

"Who?"

"I don't know. Just send someone over to 668 Tree Way!"

"Is it possible your car was towed or repossessed?"

"No!"

"When was it taken?"

"I just saw the guy drive it away!"

"What kind of car?"

"A blue Nissan."

"What direction did he go?"

"I don't know! Just send someone!"

"Hang on, I'll get someone going. Don't hang up."

"He's already gone! Just send someone over here."

"Did he have keys in the car?"

"Um. What?"

Real car thefts are actually pretty rare. I smell a rat. I ask again, "When did this happen?"

"Ten minutes ago," she tells me.

"Why did you wait so long to call?"

The squads get rolling right away, but I keep her on the line to get her name and phone number. Or at least, I try.

"What do you need that for?" she blurts out when I ask for her last name.

She is like a lot of people who want the police to just blindly go red-lights-and-sirens into a situation they know nothing about, on faith that the caller is telling the truth. *I told you it was stolen! Just go out and get it back for me!*

Then I say, "The cops are checking the area for your car. Now, were your keys inside when it was taken? How did they steal it, do you think?"

So, the cops are driving around her house with sirens blasting and she can hear them now, looking for this alleged stolen vehicle, and at last she says, "Well, my husband has a key."

"Did your husband take the car?"

"Well, maybe. We're getting a divorce and he wants the car."

Duh. By this time, she's crying. Either she is lying to me and she knows it, or her sense of denial is so strong that she is refusing to admit the truth even to herself. Either way, we've been misled. Whether it was premeditated or not, she hadn't so much called us with a crime to report, but with an agenda to fulfill. She is losing her car, and she wants us to get it back.

A good 911 call-taker can smell an agenda a mile away and let the officers know before they arrive. Some of the people I work with are absolute *masters* at this because they've heard all the bullshit lies anyone could imagine.

In fact, not only did the husband take the car, but he had a legal right to. Just that day, a family court judge had ruled that the car, among other things, belonged to her ex.

Even after all that, our caller probably hung up feeling like the police didn't give a shit about her. If you asked her today, she would tell you that the police don't care.

What can we do? Not send her a Christmas card?

* * *

People break the law hundreds of times in a hundred little ways every day and don't get caught. That drives some folks just crazy because they think police don't care. Not true. They do care. They just don't always do exactly what you think they should in order to solve crimes.

It's hard for me to get as outraged about crime as the average person does. I see it so often now. Some callers seem to sense my apathy and make it their personal mission to make me as outraged as they are.

That's usually the guy who wants to tell me the entire history of his life as it pertains to his neighbors, the high price of gas, and crime prevention in general. He's the official or unofficial leader of his neighborhood watch group, which he believes gives him the right to call 911 every other day for every minor code infraction.

This person will most likely chew on my ear for as long as it takes to get something out of me. This person doesn't just want justice, he wants validation. Sometimes I have that to give. Sometimes it feels like too much to ask. Maybe that's what burnout is. When you've run out, entirely.

On a good day, I can listen with empathy, dispatch the call, and go on with my life. On a bad day, all I can think is, *You're right sir! It's absolutely intolerable that your neighbor's dog is barking. Hold on while I divert our squads from this medical they're headed to so we can catch Spot in the act!*

When that starts to happen, I know my tank is running low. I need something to fill it back up. Something positive.

This one fills my tank for a couple of weeks:

A woman named Janet comes to the station looking for help finding her adult daughter, Jacinda. Jacinda was supposed to have flown in to the Minneapolis airport from out of state and was several hours late. Janet is deaf and doesn't know what to do to find her daughter.

One of the officers on duty knows American Sign Language, so for several minutes, I get to watch their conversation, her quick, anxious movements contrasting with his calm, reassuring ones. After Janet left, he does some checking and finds Jacinda, who is just fine and on her way to her mother's house.

Using a teletype machine—a phone with a keyboard—I get to tell Janet the good news. As we "talk," our keystrokes are recorded and printed on a ticker tape, just like a receipt.

"Your daughter is at work and she says she will come to the house at about 11:30. GA." I tap out on my keyboard. "GA" means "go ahead." It means that I'm done typing, and she can respond.

"Oh, thank you so much. I would not have been able to sleep tonight."

"You're very welcome." I finish. "We're glad to help."

After I disconnect, I take the printout of our conversation and keep it at my console for the evening.

We're glad to help.

* * *

Some people call 911 and immediately apologize for calling. "I'm sorry to call on this line, but my wife's having a stroke."

Then there's the guy who calls 911 because he wants directions to the local movie theater.

If you need police, you can call 911. Analyze whether it was truly emergent later when you're alive and safe. People ask about various hotlines that are set up to handle emergencies, like 211 for family emergencies or *77 if you're being pulled over by someone who is impersonating police. My advice to them is always just to call 911. Don't call your mom, don't call Onstar, and for God's sake don't call your friend who's a cop in another city ten miles away. If you need police, call 911.

I've never seen anyone get in trouble for using 911 on something that's less than emergent. If your emergency really isn't, the worst thing we'll do is put you on hold until we can get to you. And if you're calling for directions to the movie theater, you could be on hold for a very, very long time.

* * *

Some of the people I work with get hooked on emergency worker-type TV shows, like *Third Watch* and *ER*. *ER* had me for a while. Dr. Mark Green was my favorite character until everything bad in the world started happening to him. He found out he had brain cancer. His new wife, a surgeon, was sued for malpractice. His toddler daughter wound up in the ER after ingesting some ecstasy that she fished out of his other daughter's backpack. His good-looking doctor and nurse colleagues are also in constant crisis, one family member after another getting wheeled into the ER.

It got to be too much. People who write these shows seem to think that it's not dramatic enough for emergency workers to witness other people's tragedies every day. The tragedy has to happen to *them*.

Well, I'm here to tell you, it *is* enough. It's plenty.

The Parenting Option

On a sunny day in June, I adopt my darling stepdaughter. It is official. She is now free to do to me all the awful things that I did to my own mother. I pray that she won't, but in this job, I witness a whole range of the awful things that children do as children. Conversely, I see all the awful things that parents do as parents, and I am sometimes amazed.

My husband reassures me with the reasoning that just the fact that I worry so much about being a good mother makes me a good mother. Hmm. Not much incentive to stop worrying, though.

"911?"

"Hi, this is Jean Markus. I live at . . ."

"19114 Deercrest?"

"How did you know?"

"It's on my screen, but I recognize your voice, Jean."

"Okay, well, what I want is for a cop car and an ambulance to come and take my kids because my boyfriend says he's going to work in the morning and I threw my back out and if he goes to work, there won't be anybody taking care of them."

"Your boyfriend Travis?"

"Yeah."

"Let me get this straight. You want us to baby-sit your kids?"

"Well, when parents can't take care of their kids, don't they go into foster care or something?"

"Yes, but not for a day while your boyfriend goes to work. Foster care is long term. Do you want us to take your girls for a long time?"

"Well, I can't take care of them. I threw my back out and I don't have a job. But can they come home by the end of the week?"

"No, Jean. That's not how it would be."

"Oh." Crying. Sobbing.

"Jean?"

"If you don't take them I don't know what's going to happen!"

That's my cue to get someone over there. I put the call into the system, then Marsha keys the mike for the main channel.

"2464?"

"2464."

"For 2464 and a backup squad, head over to 19114 Deercrest. Thirty-one-year-old female says she's not well and wants us to take care of her children tomorrow. Unknown what the real issue is tonight . . . possibly a dispute with the boyfriend."

" '64 copies. I know the house."

" '64, do you want an ambulance started?"

"Negative. I'll advise."

"Thank you, 23:32."

Anyone whose address or voice we know by heart we call a "frequent flyer." Frequent flyers are people who are always in crisis. Frequent flyers are the houses where someday, something big is going to happen. Maybe a murder or a suicide, or the house burns down. And when it happens, the police say, well, this was a problem house. And then the reporters and the neighbors say, why didn't you do anything to stop it?

Or maybe nothing big happens at all. Maybe all that happens is that some poor child has a very sad and unfortunate upbringing by a mother who was too mentally ill to give her what she needed. I don't know which is worse.

* * *

The drug of choice for kids nowadays is a little white drug called methamphetamine or crystal meth. The longer I am at this job, the more I am struck by how close it is to me, my house, my now almost-teenaged daughter and the school she goes to.

I'm still somewhat puzzled by my own addiction, and I find that I am absolutely *riveted* by the phenomenon of hundreds and thousands of teenagers getting hooked on a drug that is so destructive.

The cops call them meth-heads. I begin to learn them by name. They are kids in their late teens and early twenties who live in a constant state of searching. They slowly walk away from everything of value in their lives until all that's left is the drug and the desperate pursuit of more. They age five times faster than normal, but stop maturing. They grow literal holes in their brains. They slowly stop feeling emotionally and become sociopaths. Their hearts weaken. They scratch themselves raw.

When they call for help, which is rare, I know them immediately. They often don't hear me. They ramble on and on and tell me nothing of use. They lie about what they need from me. I want to tell them things that I know, but I don't. It's not my role.

When one of them dies, some cops act like they don't feel sorry. I don't say out loud that I feel sorry, either. One less, someone might say. Even though we know for every one fewer, there are likely two more coming.

When I see their booking photos with their raw skin and their thousand-mile stares, I think: Thank God I got sober when I did.

One night, an older couple comes to the twenty-four-hour window of our dispatch center. While walking through the parking lot of the local motel, they found a small baggy with white crystals. Jody, who is in school to be a cop, recognizes it right away as crystal meth.

I've never seen it, so I cautiously lean over the baggy as she examines it. She pokes at it with her French manicure and explains to me that she knows it's meth because of the crystal texture of it, and that if it was cocaine, it would be smooth, more powdery, and matted.

I don't tell her that I could pick out cocaine in a lineup any day of the week and twice on Sunday. I am careful who I share that with. I stare at the tiny baggy in awe. This is the latest thing that kills kids. I wonder what it will be ten years from now. I wonder if I will still be sitting in this seat to witness it.

The next day, another crystal meth baggy comes in. This time, the deliverer is the mother of a fifteen-year-old girl. She has discovered a tiny plastic ziplock in her daughter's backpack. It's almost empty except for the salty white crystals in its corners.

"I want to have this tested," she tells me, smiling, embarrassed. "You know, in case it's pot or something." She slowly pushes it through the opening at the bottom of the security window that divides us.

I look up at her. She is dressed smartly. She wears a burgundy leather blazer that is so new I can smell it through the small opening in the bullet-proof glass. Her hair is styled, streaked and layered like that of a news anchor's. She knows that whatever this bag held, it wasn't pot. But maybe pot is the only thing she can wrap her head around just yet.

"I'll see if one of our detectives is available."

"Okay, thanks!"

A.J., a police detective in general investigations, has come in on a weekend day to finish up some paperwork. He takes the baggy from mom, and I can tell from the disgusted look on his face that it's probably the real deal. Now he's going to have to stay half an hour longer and write another report.

Damn kids and their meth.

Mom chats with A.J. in the lobby for a few minutes, then turns to go. I smile and wave to her, as though this is a downtown boutique and we've just sold her a lovely pair of boots to go with her new blazer. She smiles back at me as though her daughter has never used meth. And everything's going to be okay.

The Note

"911?"

"My husband's missing. He went out for a walk this morning and he's still not back."

"Does he usually take long walks?"

"Yeah, but not this long. He's got diabetes. He's got a lot of problems. Health problems."

It's only been a couple of hours, but it's not for me to decide when a man's been missing too long (or not long enough), so I put a call into the system and assure Mrs. Reese she'll be contacted soon.

I label the call as an "attempt to locate" (ATL) and not as a "missing person" call because it's not taking place under what we would normally think of as suspicious circumstances. Husbands disappear from their wives all the time, and vice versa. Mostly, by choice.

2660 must be thinking the same as I am because instead of driving out to the house, he opts to call Mrs. Reese and take the information by phone. A little while later, a general message goes out to the console of each officer and dispatcher. "Attempt to locate John Reese: 58-year-old white male, 5-foot-10, 175 pounds, gray hair, blue eyes. Last seen wearing jeans and a flannel shirt and on foot northbound from 3200 block of Terrace Hills. Unknown destination."

About forty-five minutes later, Mrs. Reese calls again.

"I want to talk to the officer who called me before, but I want him to come over here." she says. She is crying.

"Okay, did your husband get back home?"

"No," she says. "But I think I know where he is. I found a note."

Well, there you go, I figure. He left a note. Considerate.

I put another call into the system, but it takes five or ten minutes before the officer gets to it. He had to take another call. But before we get the chance to dispatch it to him, Mrs. Reese is back on the line.

"When is the officer going to come?"

"As soon as he's done with the call he's on," I say somewhat defensively. I'm not his keeper, right?

"Well, it's really important," she says.

"Okay, I'll let him know." Geez, impatient.

Thanks to Mr. Reese's note, officers were able to find him in a park about two miles from his house. He brought a gun with him on his walk and shot himself in the woods, just as his note said he would.

On Wannabes

I "meet" a lot of wannabe cops, self-appointed security guards, and real-life security guards, and none of them get a whole lot of love from me, I'm sorry to say. It's mostly because they try too hard to make me like them. But I only like cops and civilians. Anyone who thinks there is something in between is suspicious. I figure, why would anyone want to do a cop's job if he's not a cop? Because he thinks it's fun?

A wannabe cop is usually a white male in his twenties or thirties working somewhere as a security guard (sometimes real, sometimes self-appointed), and he is usually less concerned with helping the truly needy or sick than he is with righting all the wrongs of the world, like being too rich, driving too nice a car, and having too pretty a girlfriend in the passenger seat.

Wannabe cops often ride around town in old Crown Victorias they bought at police auctions, equipped with scanners and light bars that are legal to own, but not to operate, and they almost always make it some or all the way through cop school, but don't get hired by any agencies for reasons that nobody can quite put a finger on.

These are the ones who call us as they're burning Mach 10 down the highway, one hand on the wheel, one hand on the phone, screaming out license plates and asking for a "black and white" on westbound Highway X at the Y exit.

"911?"

"Okay, write down this plate. Kilo Charlie Bravo, five, six, five. Got that?"

"Roger Wilko. What's your emergency, sir?"

"I'm following a guy who's doing at least eighty miles an hour and he was tailgating me big-time before that. Then he passed me and flipped me off! How fast can you get an officer out here?"

"How fast are *you* going?"

"I have to go fast to keep up with this guy so you can catch him."

"Well, stop. All our cars are tied up, and you're not legal to speed either."

"What are you going to do?"

"We're going to check the area as soon as a squad clears."

"He's going to be gone by then."

"You're probably right, and that's unfortunate. Do you want an officer to call you and make a written complaint?" Which will go absolutely nowhere because it's his word against yours?

"Yes, I do." Of course you do, Mr. Wrong-righter.

"Are you still following?"

"Yeah, but, I mean, he's going to kill somebody."

"And so might you, if you don't slow down. Do you understand me?"

Pause. "Copy."

I know of one guy, a local security guard, who actually used to pull people over with his "squad." His "career" ended when he pulled over an off-duty chief of police. In his defense, he never ticketed anyone. Verbal warnings only. I'm sure this mattered big time at the sentencing hearing.

Self-appointed security guards (SASGs) run the gamut from old geezer neighborhood watchers to housewives with a lot of free time. They are usually protecting some small community living area that sees a moderate amount of crime, like an apartment building or a trailer court. SASGs appear to be motivated by some previous incident in their lives, when something very unfair happened, something they always wanted to make right. Maybe they were bullied in school. Maybe they had a bike stolen and never got it back.

SASGs are hyper-aware of all the awful things that go on in the world. But unlike most people, they are unable to resist fighting every single battle, large and small, and it's, well, a *big job*. And they want the police to fight every little battle like it's a big battle, and police don't like to be told how to do anything, thank you very much, and neither do dispatchers, just for the record.

SASGs are duty bound and righteous, and they call about every little suspicious thing. They call so often that their voices tend to shut something off in our heads. It's the switch that makes us willing to be open to whatever emergency our caller is calling to report. It is triggered by the way they always identify themselves as if we are longtime buddies, united in a common purpose: to rid the city of all teenagers, fast cars, and loud mufflers. These calls are almost always about nothing more than minor violations, and our response to these violations is almost always inadequate by their standards.

"911?"

"Yeah, this is Steve, you know, the security guard at Manor Community?" Steve is not employed by any person or entity, neither as a security guard nor anything else, and when I found this out after nine months of taking his calls, I felt entirely ripped off.

"Yeah, Steve, what can I do for you?"

"There was a bunch of boys out here fighting in the park area."

"Are they still there, fighting?"

"No, but I'm following one of 'em in my truck. The cops know my truck, it's the old red one."

"Is anyone hurt?"

"I don't think so . . ."

"Do you know who they are?"

"Oh, yeah, they live down the street."

"Then you should stop following. There's no need."

"Well, uh, we should have someone come out here and talk to 'em."

"Okay, why don't you head back to the trailer park and I'll have a squad meet you there."

"Who's coming, Officer Jim?"

"Uh, possibly. Whoever's free."

"Maybe Rocco?"

"Whoever clears from the medical they're on."

"Oh, sure. Okay."

SASGs pride themselves in knowing as many of our officers by name as possible, and they also like to do their level best to establish a rapport with the dispatchers they talk to. But I can't help it, the more an SASG tries to endear him or herself to me, the oogier I get. Same goes for wannabes. Sorry. Every day, all day, we are burdened with knowing all about the worst possible things that people do to others and to themselves. Wannabes and SASGs go *looking* for the shit. It's not even a paid job for them; it's a hobby, a passion. I don't get that.

Real security guards can be okay, as long as they are in touch with their status as nothing more than a warm body in a uniform, with no authority and no real purpose except to be a visual deterrent. Department stores hire security guards to protect their product, and this is a good thing, as long as the guards know that there's a limit to what lengths a person should go to in order to recover a six-dollar tube of lipstick.

In my opinion, said six-dollar tube of lipstick is not worth chasing the sixteen-year-old suspect for ten minutes on foot and getting into a fight with her, which ends in an incident report and having to get a tetanus shot when she scratches you because she was at this point scared to death of the crazed, panting security guard who had followed her for ten minutes over nothing but a lousy six-dollar tube of lipstick.

Yet we get plenty of calls from security guards in midrun, pursuing some poor slob with a candy bar, or worse yet, someone who tried to steal something but failed, and is now a failure *and* the subject of a foot chase.

Listen, Sparky, if the suspect dumped the Vanilla Ice CD in the parking lot, pick the blasted thing up and take it as a win for the home team. Don't give chase for *nothing*. You have no gun. You have no backup. You have no training. (*And yes,* I'm aware of the mandatory verbal judo class JCPenney made you take). And now you're going to get your ass kicked because the suspect has more to lose than you do. You could call 911, but a good ass-whooping can easily happen within the four to five minutes you'll have before the cops get there. And if the cops went red-lights-and-sirens to get to you in four minutes, it's because they were worried about saving *your* dumb ass, not about the Vanilla Ice CD.

Of course, I know how judgmental this all sounds. But here's why we care so much about all this: This is the kind of stuff that gets people hurt or killed over nothing. That's all. We don't want *anybody* killed. Not cops, not civilians, and not wannabes, SASGs, and security guards. Not even someone who would shoplift a Vanilla Ice CD.

DOA

Chad insists it's not true, but our dispatch center has mice.

This is no surprise to those of us in dispatch who are also good little housewives and like to keep our clean little houses *just so.* We know the pitfalls of poor housekeeping. We see the dust and the crumbs that sit for weeks and months, and *cringe.*

Most workplaces get cleaned on the weekends, when everyone is gone. But our room is never empty . . . not at night, not on holidays, not ever. And we never leave the comm center to eat, so neither do our crumbs.

The janitor, a somewhat angry (yet surprisingly personable) guy named Gordy, comes in once a day on weekdays to empty the garbage cans, talk to Leo, the daytime supervisor, about various things that piss him off, and distractedly push a carpet sweeper across our matted, stained carpet. The carpet sweeper has almost no useful purpose except to exonerate the county from what could otherwise be described as the *total* neglect of our work space. When Gordy leaves, there is still *plenty* left over for the mice.

Lily calls the comm center a petri dish. It's a ripe little bucket of whatever is left from all of us eating and talking and spitting and farting 24 hours a day, 365 days a year. Mix it all together with almost no meaningful ventilation . . . and voila! You have the funk of dispatch.

Every once in a while, one of us (usually one of the married ladies) just gets fed up, takes the old sky-blue canister-style vacuum cleaner out of the janitor's closet, and rolls it into the comm center. It has to be a quiet night, or maybe a quiet Sunday morning, for this to happen. The vacuum (circa maybe 1977) is too loud to put up with while answering phones and talking on the main.

It's music to my ears, listening to all the popcorn shells, cookie crumbs, pebbles. and whatnot get sucked into the vacuum tube and out of the room. *Our room.* Where we spend almost every minute of every eight-hour day, except when we're in the john staring at the old floor tiles, which are also never clean.

Once, on day shift, Jean detected an *unfamiliar* odor coming from console 36. After rolling away the file cabinets, pulling the power cords away, and shining a flashlight into the abyss below the desk, she found a body, DOA. It was a deceased mouse in a forgotten trap.

The Job

I'm not working toward anyone's bottom line in what I do. I'm not making widgets for some CEO who has a cabin in Aspen, six Jet Skis, and a designer dog, and I'm not waiting for a raise every six months just to see if I'm worth anything in his eyes. I just work for the next man or woman who calls on the phone and asks me for help. That fact alone makes me love this job.

I believe that there is a God, but that He can't be blamed for all the times that people hurt people. I believe that God loves his children, but He can only do so much for them and to them without stepping on their free will.

I pray to God very often to work through me. God helps me to help people I don't want to, people I may think don't deserve it. On a good day, I let God make all my decisions, I have compassion, and I don't judge.

Because of this job, every day that I come home to my normal, healthy family, I thank God. I thank God that when my husband and I argue, it doesn't get personal or violent. That when I come home from work, he's there, just reading the paper, missing me. He has not been drinking for the last five hours and waiting to start a fight. We live together because we want to, not because we have to, just to get by.

I thank God that my daughter doesn't smart off to me or swear at me, as so many kids do, that the biggest crime she's ever committed was to scribble in her math textbook, and that when she got in trouble, she felt remorse. She talks to us, and she likes school. She doesn't get into fights or take guns to school. She doesn't lash out.

I thank God for my parents. Despite all my mistakes, they still care for and support me. I'm grateful that when we talk, it's because we want to, not because we have some bizarre obligation to. The idea of a fistfight breaking out at Thanksgiving dinner is about as likely as a meteor landing on my Mom and Dad's front yard. I thank God that despite all my faults, in their eyes I'm just about perfect.

Because of this job, I don't have to wonder what my life would be like if I didn't have parents and a husband and daughter who love me. I see examples of how that would go every single day.

* * *

Some operators freeze when things heat up. Maybe an officer calls out for help on the main channel, and instead of acting, the operator goes completely blank. Maybe a caller says "My husband just shot himself," and the operator can't think of what to say.

This happens to me sometimes, and it can happen to some who have worked 911 for twenty-five years, though they are not likely to admit it. No one has ever died or been hurt because of a freeze on my part. But worrying about that possibility sometimes keeps me up at night.

Turnover is rare. Despite the shitty hours and the stress, it still pays better than most other jobs with similarly shitty hours and stress, like, say, waiting tables or sorting mail. A few weeks after we lost Sela, I start hearing rumblings about a new girl.

All I know about Sela's departure is that nobody will say anything directly about it. She seemed fine, yet I always heard rumors that she wasn't. I even heard Kristen say very loudly that Sela just couldn't do the job. A harsh indictment, indeed. I feared that the same was said about me behind my back.

Then one day, I saw Sela freeze up. I don't even remember what the call was. Doesn't matter. What matters is that even with Marlys telling her exactly what to do, what buttons to push, what to say, all of it, she got stuck in her head. She didn't do what Marlys told her. If fact, she didn't do *anything*.

Within a couple of weeks, Sela was transferred to an admin job downtown. Everybody was a little bit frosted about that, because we heard she didn't have to take a cut in pay. If there's anything that helps us slog along in here, it's the feeling that what we do is harder and worth more money than typing memos and making copies.

I don't know if I believe she actually got no cut in pay

and weekends off. Still, no more 911. Wouldn't you miss that? God bless Sela. Sometimes, mostly when I'm working on a sunny Saturday afternoon, I get a little jealous.

Then they hired Jo. The first thing I did when I met Jo was to bombard her with all my thoughts about the job: that training was the hardest thing you'll ever go through, that it was totally natural to feel completely overwhelmed, and that I knew exactly how she was feeling. There, I thought. Now she won't have any more stress.

Jo was in school for law enforcement, with the goal of becoming an officer. When she spoke to you face to face, her voice was normal. When it came time to dispatch on the fire channel, her voice turned into a balloon letting its air out in slow, painful gasps.

I also heard rumors that she didn't listen to Lily. Tried to do things her way. Whatever you do when you're new, ya *gotta* listen to Lily. Geez. Do things your way ten years from now when you actually know what you're doing. She lasted just a few weeks. I guess it's not for everybody.

Every once in a while, someone will ask me whether they think so-and-so should try out for an open dispatcher spot. All I can do is shrug. Don't even know how I got here, really. And I don't know what those who hired me saw either. Chad did mention once that he liked that I had a college degree. That makes me laugh. Which class would it have been that prepared me for the main? Which class did I take that prepared me for domestics, suicidal people, fatal accidents? Was it the semester I spent studying *Paradise Lost*? Or perhaps Intro to Watercolor?

All I know about dispatchers is in the small set of statistics that surrounds me every day. Of the dispatchers at county, there are four men and eighteen women. Two of the men and one of the women aspire to be cops. The rest of us like it just fine behind the phone, thank you very much. (I can just see me in uniform, 9-millimeter in hand, yelling, "Stop, or I'll wet myself!")

Some of us are college grads, but most aren't. I'm the only former reporter my dispatch center has seen, I know that for sure. It doesn't take a rocket scientist to do this job, yet I also think it's one of the hardest jobs you can have. It takes a special person.

A lot of people think that if you can't hack it in dispatch, you could never make it as a cop. That would imply that being a cop is more challenging than being a dispatcher, or that being a dispatcher is just a stepping stone to being a cop. Either way, cops tend to make more money than dispatchers, which nobody seems to question. It's that whole "putting your life on the line" thing, apparently.

When I tell strangers that I work as a 911 dispatcher, they tend to look surprised. I don't think it's that I *don't* look like one, but more the question of, *what does one of those look like?*

Retirement

When Kristen announces her retirement, I think I feel relief. I think so because I've expected to feel that way for so long. Seems like every time I had a rough night with her, there was always someone around who would remind me, "Don't worry about her. She's going to retire soon, anyway."

Kristen's pending retirement is why I so often fail to speak my mind to her. Why, when I'm mad, I just suck it up. I tell myself, she's leaving soon. Why rock the boat?

Each day, when I arrive at work, I look for her car. If it's there, I know what kind of day I'm likely to have. I've grown to hate her car, some kind of silver GM product with rounded bumpers and a dark interior. It reminds me of how many mistakes I make and how many I have left to make. It reminds me that no matter what you do, some people don't want to be happy. It reminds me that even when it means my very sanity, I can't seem to stand up for myself worth a shit. And then when I'm done not standing up for myself, I can't let it go.

Whatever I feel for Kristen from one day to the next, it's my own inability to deal with conflict that I hate the most. I've told everyone who would listen that I wasn't going to let Kristen get away with her snide remarks, her unreasonable perfectionism. I was going to shove it all back in her face by reporting her to Chad each time. How empowering. I wasn't going to build a wall, I was going to *change the system.*

Yet, every day I work with her, she remains the same, while I grow into an emotional wreck. I don't need to build a wall, and I can't change the system. I need to get a life.

Now she's retiring.

It happens just like that. I have been praying for it all along, but when she announces it, just before summer, our busiest time, I am numb.

The news travels fast. Chad says he hopes she'll work part-time, so we won't be short-staffed. Mel says she will miss her, that she was never that scared of her. Shawn says she's the best dispatcher he has ever worked with. It turns into a funeral, in which the deceased, regardless of what kind of life he or she led, becomes sainted in death.

It climaxes on her last day. Sitting at her throne on the last afternoon shift of her life, Kristen is surrounded by flowers from well-wishers. There are cards strewn about and there's a cake from a McGlynn's bakery with colored, flowered frosting. Kristen is saying good-bye to people she's worked with for almost thirty-four years. They are a family. I realize that I am not as much a part of that. In order to be, I would have to work the job for half a lifetime, too. I don't know if I want that. I don't want to burn out and keep working, to have newcomers pray for my retirement day.

But the people who will miss her most are the officers who relied on her calm, self-assured voice broadcasting over the main channel every day. They trusted her. No matter what was going on at their end, the officers could always count on her to be fast, accurate, and comprehensible. She didn't care whose feelings she hurt to make sure that was always the case. In law enforcement, some of the things that make you good at your job are also the things that drive people away.

Just before she is set to leave for the evening, and forever, Lily announces Kristen's retirement on the main: "Information for Ramsey County: Kristen Miller is retiring today after thirty-three years, ten months, and two weeks. We thank her for her service and . . . we will miss her."

Lily breaks up a little at the end.

I feel so confused. There are tears in my eyes, but I don't shed them. I know they aren't coming for the same reason as anyone else's. Or maybe they are. Ugh. A whole day devoted to someone who made me miserable. I only ever looked at that side of it. I haven't been there long enough to really appreciate her service, or to become her friend.

But worse than that, I had never had the guts to just tell her to kiss my ass when I needed to. She would have respected that. But not on her last day. The chance to "grow some balls" (as my husband would say) is gone.

I need some kind of ending even if it's shitty. So I find her just as she and Casey are lugging all her booty out to her car. I give her a hug. I don't know what else to do, and I know she isn't going to do it if I don't.

She hugs me back, and we aren't awkward. She tells me: "Go to graduate school, like you talked about. Don't be here in thirty years."

I had forgotten I'd told her about that. It wasn't something I'd shared with a lot of people.

Don't be here in thirty years. I don't know if she means that I'm not right for the job, or that she wishes she had done something different with *her* thirty-three years.

I guess I'll know in about thirty years.

Wherever You Go

After Kristen is gone, things are just as I imagined they could be, only different. I still suck at the main channel, I'm still working afternoons, and I'm still me. Maybe that's what gets me thinking that I need to leave. With Kristen gone, I'm the only one left to point out my own shortcomings. I do my best to compensate for her.

Wherever I go, there I am.

Besides that, nothing is happening. The calls keep coming in, but nothing exciting, life-changing, sweat-inducing . . . ever . . . seems . . . to happen anymore.

Lily seems to think something big *is* coming. Something that was making the hairs on her neck stand up. Some nights, I sit on pins and needles and thinking that same thing. It has been too quiet a summer. And though that is, in general, a good thing to have, it leaves me wondering, "When will *it* happen?" Because when *it* does, I don't want to be caught off guard.

In this job, some of us develop instincts. Feelings. One night, Gina took at call from a gas-station customer who said she saw two young black males wearing rubber gloves enter as she was leaving. No other information.

Casey, who's got about three years on the job, overheard this, then when he heard the 911 line ring, he saw Mel reach for it. Mel is barely out of training, and Casey's instincts told him that this next call would be from the gas station, so he told her to let him pick it up. He was right.

And despite all of Casey's efforts to move quickly, the two men robbed the store, pistol-whipped the clerk, and got away.

I wasn't there for that one, and, oddly, that pisses me off. Sometimes, I find that I *want* something big to happen. This strange new need I have developed is rarely ever satisfied. It's the need to feel the blood pumping, all over, in my head, my wrists, my ankles. It's a need to catch a bad guy, or to dispatch a fully involved house fire. To be *necessary*. To feel like I'm something more than a police department secretary who works nights, weekends, and holidays. Every once in a while, we get a theft-in-progress that leads to a little bit of a foot chase, which can be kinda fun. But, for months on end, all I seem to get are busy-work calls.

Break-ins, recovered property, stolen cars, runaway tenth-graders, lost dogs. Blaaaaah blah blah blah blah. The job is filled with this type of thing, over and over, day after day. Victims of mid- to low-level crimes, in my observation, are often far more irritable than victims of high-level or violent crime. They have had more time to think about how badly they've been wronged. They don't get enough validation from anyone around them about how badly they've been wronged. Often, they are people who hang out with criminals and drug addicts, then can't believe it when they wake up one day to find the TV gone. They won't let up until the crime has been solved. They leave message on top of message. They want to kill the message-taker. Me.

They call and call. They don't want to hold, thank you very much. They don't want the answer you give them. They don't want to be called back, they want satisfaction right now. They want us to fingerprint this, investigate that, possibly send over some cross-eyed detective in a trench coat, who will exact a confession from the shifty-eyed butler.

Worse than the victims of crime-lite are the mothers and girlfriends of the men who get arrested. They are the caretakers after the crisis, and almost worse than the wife-beaters and meth-heads they love so devotedly.

"He can't go more than two hours in jail without his asthma meds!" one of them cries to me one night. That's funny, he just stayed up on meth and booze for three days straight and somehow managed to survive without his inhaler—and to fight with the arresting officer.

"They towed my son's car for no good reason. They're just picking on him. He doesn't drink that much anymore." Lemme guess. He only had two beers. And if the car is so blessed important, why can't he call for it himself?

Sometimes I think it is this type of work that creates the bitterness and cynicism we tend to suffer from. Maybe it's not the big stuff that only comes once in a while, but the little stuff that drips and drips and drips on our foreheads like Chinese water torture. When we are not answering emergency calls, sometimes we are just the bearers of mediocre news, and the dispatchers of mediocre calls, to cops who feel the same way we do. Day after day. Eight hours at a time.

I start talking myself out of it. I start disliking my callers, my coworkers. Every little call that's not an emergency grates deeply on my nerves. I start burning out. I start looking elsewhere.

Then I get a better offer. My husband tells me I can work at home, for his locksmithing business. It would be tight, but I would have a lot more freedom and I'd see Lucy a lot more. I start thinking about going back to school. I start painting the grass greener and greener. I'll make my own hours. I'll be happier.

I can't do *this job* for the rest of my life, that's for sure.

One night, I take a medical call. A forty-year-old male has fallen off the roof of his house. Conscious and breathing. I put in a call, Marsha sends police, and I dispatch the ambulance with the wife still on the line.

I think about Joe Wilson. I know that if I leave, there will never have to be another Joe Wilson to live through. At least, not for me.

I am invited on a boat outing one Sunday afternoon. It is breezy, mid-70s, and there is not a cloud in the sky, but I am on the schedule to work 3:00 to 11:00 PM. I call in sick. It is midsummer and I'm so damn sick of watching my friends and family go off to bonfires and pool parties . . . well . . . that's how I justify it.

Unfortunately, the lake my friends choose to go out on

is patrolled by none other than the deputies that I am supposed to be dispatching to. As far as I know, I am never spotted. At some point I realize, maybe I am trying to get fired. I have begun to tell myself that I could take the job or leave it. Mostly, I just couldn't spend another sunny day in the dark, musty comm center.

Though I make it through without getting busted, my day on the boat is a waste. I can't enjoy the day, floating in my little inner tube on the lake; I am too worried. The people I let down by going on my little day trip are my partners in dispatch, my friends. What if something big happened, and I wasn't there to help?

And what if the boat I was on was involved in an accident? Whom do you suppose I would have to call?

* * *

After two years on the job, I quit.

On my last day, Lily brings in a cake. She gives me a card saying it was an honor to work with me. In a few weeks, she will finally going to India to adopt her daughter. Her daughter will consume her whole life, in a magical and terrifying way. She will take a six-month leave of absence, unsure if she really ever plans to come back.

I sit next to Marsha on the main for my last eight hours. We dispatch on a domestic, a couple of bogus alarms, and a medical at the senior high-rise. One officer on the street sends me an e-mail thanking me for my service. At the end of the eighth hour, I feel relieved and sad. Nothing big or memorable has happened. At least not today.

Full Circle

For about seven months, when people ask me what I do, I hesitate, then reluctantly tell them I'm a locksmith. I only know about half of what you need to know to be a fully certified locksmith. I'm a half-breed. Again.

I spend my days opening locked cars, making appointments for my husband to do the more complicated lockwork, and keeping up with an endless mound of business-related paperwork. When I'm not doing that, I'm writing about 911. When I'm not doing that, I'm trying to steal bike rides, suppers, and walks with my daughter, who is growing up way too fast. I take a couple of math classes over the winter, then drop out because I'm too busy.

Then my husband, who switches careers almost as

much as I do, decides to close the shop. Business is declining, I'm the only employee he can afford, and our hearts just aren't in it. Jim goes back to school. I start applying for jobs here and there, but it's slim pickings. Though it's only been a few years since I worked as a reporter, that seems like a lifetime ago. The only thing I know how to do anymore is the thing I never thought I was any good at.

I'm a 911 dispatcher.

* * *

I get hired right out of the gate. In fact, because I've got some experience, I get job offers from two agencies in the same week, both city dispatch centers. Each police department puts me through a little bit of a background investigation, of course.

The White Bear Lake Police Department asks for a short biography. I write a one-page e-mail about how I grew up in White Bear Lake, graduated from the hometown high school, then smoked a lot of crack. I went to treatment. Later, I met the man I would marry. I went to college, then started and quit a bunch of jobs. I adopted a little girl, my stepdaughter, who is, I must say, wonderful. The end.

I am in Target looking for a new pair of sandals and a sports bra when the detective who has been tasked with "backgrounding" me calls me on my cell phone. He is a little curious about the whole *smoking crack* thing. I give him the edited-for-TV version, ending with how I went to treatment. All the while, I am pushing a cart and checking out the latest in plastic thongs. (In the *shoe* section.) Our conversation is short. The detective seems largely disinterested in my sordid past, like he's just checking off boxes.

The best thing about this time around is that I don't care as much. I know all the good and bad. I figure, if I'm supposed to take the job again, it will come to me like it did before. If not, maybe I could settle for doing something less horrible, something less wonderful.

Of the two job offers I receive, I pick the one closest to my house.

I get stuck on afternoons, of course.

* * *

White Bear Lake is a whole other animal, whatever that means. For the city of about 25,000, there is only one dispatcher. This person takes the 911 and non-911 calls, dispatches police, fire, and medical emergencies, runs warrant checks, and enters all the stolen and missing items and people into the system. When the shit hits the fan, it all sprays in one direction.

There is no safety net at White Bear Lake, so even though I spend the first several weeks with a trainer by my side, I do my best to pretend I am alone.

Sometimes, hours and hours go by and nothing interesting happens. Sergeant Gregory stops in and talks about the cross-dressing shoplifter they caught at the local Kmart. He says, *he* stuffed all the *makeup* in *his purse.* The *he* took his *purse* and left the store.

When there's time, I drill my trainer, Wendy, on all that can go wrong (and most certainly will) during the course of a shift. If we get a chase, how do I switch to the statewide channel? How do I dispatch White Bear main and the statewide channel at the same time? What if we get a tornado? What if the computers crash? All these things were taken care of for me at the county, by people who were clearly more capable than I. The idea that an entire dispatch center will be entrusted to me would be entirely amusing if it wasn't so downright frightening.

I wish Kristen could see me now. She wouldn't believe it. Not only am I *dispatching* on the main; I *am* the main. I am the Lord your Dispatcher. Let's pray to God I don't fuck it up.

"911?"

"Oh my God you gotta get over here right now!"

"What's wrong?"

"He's hitting me! He's hitting me and he won't leave me alone!"

"Are there any weapons?"

"Oh God oh God."

"Are there any weapons?"

"No!"

"Stay on the phone, I'm going to get the squads going."

"600 to 655 and 650?"

I get them both rolling, then somebody calls on the non-emergency line.

"WhiteBearLakePoliceandFireisthisanemergency?"

"Well . . . I guess . . . not really."

"Please hold!"

Blam.

"Julie, are you still with me?"

"Yeeeeeeehhhhhs." Hysterical crying.

"Where is he now?"

"I . . . think . . . he's . . . in the basement."

"Does he drive?"

"No. He has a bike."

"A bicycle?"

"The cops are here!"

"Okay . . ." Click.

I release the one call, and another line lights up.

"911?"

"There's two guys fighting on County Road J and St. Ivan Street. You better get over here before they kill each other."

"Any weapons?"

"No."

"Hang on. Don't hang up, okay, sir?"

Shit. 656 is on lunch break at his house. Not anymore.

"600 to 656."

Heavy sigh on the main. "656 here."

"Check for a domestic between two males at County Road J and St. Ivan. No weapons."

"Copy."

"Is there a squad to back?"

I can see none on my screen, but maybe if I sound desperate enough, I can scare up a lieutenant or a school resource officer with a minute to spare.

"658 . . . I'll go."

Disco!

Another 911 line lights up. Another passing motorist to tell me about the male/male fight. I put him on hold.

Another on the non-emergency line.

"WhiteBearLakePoliceandFireisthisanemergency?"

Blam. Another blinking line, pardon my French.

Back on the main: "655 to 600 . . . run our suspect for warrants, please."

You betcha. I'll do that in my spare time.

I turn to the third of three monitors that sit in front of me, so I can run the girlfriend beater for warrants, but the system has logged me off. The 20 seconds it takes to log back on are too long for 655. He's calling for his warrant info before I even have the guy's name entered.

The state computer finally spits it out. I turn, perhaps too quickly, back toward the microphone, so I can give 655 what he needs.

I feel a snap across my chest, then a draft. The latch on my front-hook bra has come undone.

With my elbows firmly fastened to my ribs, I answer 655: "Your . . . party is clear."

"10-4."

"13:45."

The squads at the male/female domestic call for a 10-33 (emergency traffic only) on the main, while they check the basement for the girlfriend beater. For me, this means two things: The first is that I will have to dispatch briefly on two different frequencies in case any of the other officers call out on channel 2 instead of the main. The second is that I will not be able to leave the room to tuck *the girls* back in for at least another couple of minutes.

I keep my movements small and hope that my wardrobe malfunction isn't visible from under my black polyester uniform shirt. Of course, because it's shift change, there are now two other dispatchers, one sergeant, and a captain all shuffling around the small dispatch center. My luck.

"655 to 600. Cancel the 10-33. Suspect's GOA."

"Copied. Canceling the 10-33 . . . resuming normal traffic at 13:52." I swivel my elbows and the rest of me around until I am facing Naomi, my replacement. "Bathroom," I say simply.

She nods. It's as if she knows.

* * *

I quickly realize that White Bear Lake PD is every bit as short-staffed, harried, backstabbing, and marred by political, bureaucratic bullshit as the sheriff's office was. I feel at home immediately. There is infighting. There is indating. There are deep friendships and there are longstanding loyalties. There's popcorn from the bingo hall every Thursday and brownies from Sam's Club every Friday. There are long hours of boredom followed by long minutes of chaos. I am back on the roller coaster.

As in most such public service–type jobs, my first year is considered a "probation" of sorts. As if there aren't enough important reasons to want to do a good job, there is one more item that drives me: This is my hometown. I graduated from the high school, played softball in all the parks, and learned to drive my first stick shift on these streets. My parents' house and my own home, though not in the city limits, sit two blocks away from the areas that White Bear Lake police patrol.

Even more than at county, I am catering to my neighbors and to people I've known all my life. My second day on the job, I send the fire department to put out a fully engulfed pickup truck on McClellan Road. When I run the plates, I see that the registered owner is my ninth-grade homeroom teacher. Some time during week two, a motorist calls on 911 to report an erratic driver on Highway 45. I spend about five minutes on the phone with the caller, who follows behind the suspect vehicle until we get it pulled over. At the end of the call, when I ask him his name for the report, I realize he's the guy who trimmed our trees last summer.

We get a call asking for a welfare check on a thirty-year-old male who is having a nervous breakdown and drives a blue truck. I went to school with that guy. I don't get his name from the caller, but it doesn't matter. I know who he is from just the address I send the ambulance to.

Someday, I swear, I'm going to move out of this town. I'm tired of knowing everybody's little secrets. I can't even take a walk anymore without passing ten houses that I've sent police to for some medical or domestic or other. I'll wait for Lucy to graduate high school, of course.

Or maybe, someday, I'll quit for good.

Entering yet another chapter in a life stuffed with self-induced new chapters, I can only make myself one promise, that maybe I'll stop thinking so hard about whether it makes me perfectly happy, and just let it be what it is. A job.

* * *

One summer day, still not fully trained (really, what is fully trained?) but no longer in training, I experience my first big thunderstorm working dispatch at White Bear Lake. I am alone when the shit hits the fan. The storm comes fast, lasts about an hour, then lifts. Trees fall, power lines light fires, cars slide off the road, and the dispatch center explodes with calls on the phone and the radio.

Whether it is that bad a storm compared to others, I don't know. Whether I do anything right or wrong, I don't know. Nobody dies or gets injured, anyway. All fires are put out. All callers are taken care of, I think. By the end of the shift, I have aired more fire runs than I can remember, fielded more phone calls than I can count, and dispatched a domestic and a medical to boot. I am wrecked. It's too much for one person to handle alone. I think, *if this is how it's gonna be, I just don't know. This is ridiculous. It's insanity!* Familiar feelings. I want out.

I leave for the day without saying much to anyone. I would like to pull away. I would like to never hear another 911 phone ring, another transmission on the main. Another call for help.

I take my regular two days off and come back to find an e-mail from Sergeant Gregory. In it, he tells me that I handled the storm like a pro. He has copied my bosses—a supervisor, a chief, and a captain—on this glowing account of one of my worst days ever. This has apparently touched off a big ol' love fest because beneath the first note, I find three more e-mails from the higher-ups thanking me for my good work.

I am appalled that they would pull such an underhanded stunt to get me to stay after a day like that. I am also flattered and touched. I vow to hang on a little while longer. At least until something "better" comes along, right? I won't leave on a full tank.

Besides, I like helping people.

ACKNOWLEDGMENTS

Everyone I've worked with in this job has had a part in helping me learn it. Every dispatcher and every cop I've known has stories that deserve to be told. I feel fortunate to be able to tell a few of mine.

In writing this book, I changed most of the names of friends, family, and coworkers to protect their privacy. As for the callers, patients, suspects, and anyone else described in this book, all names and addresses have been changed to protect identities. In some cases, I altered other specific details and descriptors, also to protect the identities of the innocent and . . . otherwise.

My eternal gratitude goes out to my former co-workers at Ramsey County and those I now work with at White Bear Lake Police and Fire, who continually show me how the job gets done with compassion, skill, and speed. Special thanks to the three dispatch goddesses who took the time to contribute their personal thoughts and experiences to this book: Julia Mosby, Meghan Kane, and Denise Urmann. Thanks also to Valerina, for working the night the pig lady called.

Thank you to Ann Regan, editor in chief at Borealis Books, who saw what this could be even before I did, then used her editing superpowers and limitless patience to guide it toward what it is. Thanks to Alison Vandenberg, director of marketing, for putting a vibrant face on my work and presenting it with energy and style. Thanks also to Greg Britton, publisher, and to the entire staff at Borealis Books.

I would only be half the writer if not for The Loft Literary Center of Minneapolis, Jerod Santek, Alison McGhee, Molly Peacock, Evelina Chao, and my dear eleven *Loftees* (you know who you are).

And lastly, this book would not be this book without support and sacrifice from family and friends who indulge me and encourage me endlessly: Jim. Jim. Jim. Mariah. Mom and Dad. Dave and Avisia. Kellie. Marie. Rick and Renae.

Caroline Burau is a 911 dispatch operator
who lives in White Bear Lake, Minnesota.

ANSWERING 911: *Life in the Hot Seat* was designed and set in type at Borealis Books by Will Powers. The types are Franklin Gothic and Monticello. This book was printed by Thomson-Shore, Inc., Dexter, Michigan.

CPSIA information can be obtained
at www.ICGtesting.com
Printed in the USA
JSHW021000280520
5928JS00001B/75